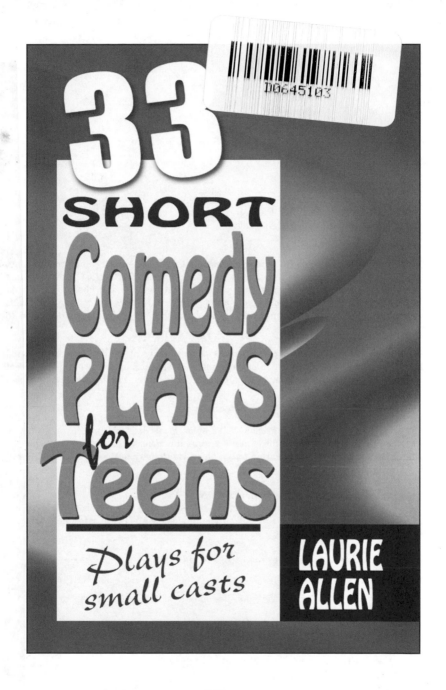

33
SHORT
Comedy
PLAYS
for
Teens

Plays for small casts

LAURIE ALLEN

mp
MERIWETHER PUBLISHING LTD.
Colorado Springs, Colorado

Meriwether Publishing Ltd., Publisher
PO Box 7710
Colorado Springs, CO 80933-7710

www.meriwether.com

Editor: Theodore O. Zapel
Assistant editor: Amy Hammelev
Cover design: Jan Melvin

Library of Congress Cataloging-in-Publication Data

Allen, Laurie, 1962-
    33 short comedy plays for teens : plays for small casts / by Laurie Allen.
-- 1st ed.
        p. cm.
    ISBN 978-1-56608-181-8
    1. Young adult drama, American. I. Title. II. Title: Thirty-three short comedy plays for teens.
    PS3601.L4324A22 2011
    812'.6--dc23

                                              2011032375

1   2   3   11   12   13

Table of Contents

1. Student Counselor

CAST: (3M, 3F) OLIVIA, JAMES, RACHEL, ERIC, MRS.
  CARSON, MR. FRASER
PROPS: Tissues
SETTING: Counselor's office

1 *(At rise, OLIVIA sits at a table. JAMES enters, a bit*
2 *distraught.)*
3 **OLIVIA: May I help you?**
4 **JAMES: I need to talk to the counselor.**
5 **OLIVIA: Mrs. Sweeney is out of the office. But I'm filling in**
6   **for her. Is there something I can help you with?**
7 **JAMES: You're filling in for Mrs. Sweeney?**
8 **OLIVIA: That's correct.**
9 **JAMES: But you're a student.**
10 **OLIVIA: Yes, but I've been Mrs. Sweeney's assistant for two**
11   **years now. And I've had the opportunity to watch her**
12   **counsel hundreds of students, with every problem**
13   **imaginable, if I might add. So, Mrs. Sweeney decided**
14   **that instead of leaving her office unattended, she**
15   **would trust me to fill in for her. She didn't want to**
16   **leave the students unable to vent in case a crisis**
17   **surfaced.**
18 **JAMES: So I have to tell *you* my problems?**
19 **OLIVIA: It's your decision, but I'm your only option for**
20   **today.**
21 **JAMES: This seems weird. And don't we have pre-cal**
22   **together?**
23 **OLIVIA: I believe so. Mr. Stuart's class. Fifth period. But I**
24   **won't be there today. Today I'm a counselor. So, how**
25   **may I help you?**
26 **JAMES: Well ...**
27 **OLIVIA: And let me remind you this is strictly confidential.**
28 **JAMES: That's good.**

1   OLIVIA: Why don't you sit down?

2   JAMES: *(Sits down.)* Thanks. I'm just curious. Are you

3   getting paid for this?

4   OLIVIA: No. But I do get extra credit.

5   JAMES: Oh. That's good.

6   OLIVIA: So go ahead. Tell me your problem.

7   JAMES: *(Deep breath)* The problem is ...

8   OLIVIA: Yes?

9   JAMES: I have a fear of speaking.

10 OLIVIA: You have a fear of speaking? But you're speaking

11   right now.

12 JAMES: Public speaking.

13 OLIVIA: Oh, public speaking. Well, that's one of the most

14   common fears that people have.

15 JAMES: At least I'm not alone out there.

16 OLIVIA: You're not. And to make you feel better, let me just

17   point out that you are not an important person.

18 JAMES: What? That's supposed to make me feel better?

19 OLIVIA: James, think about it. You're not the class

20   president. You're not on the student council. You're

21   not the class favorite. And you're not in charge of any

22   committee or organization here at school. So unless

23   you're planning to run for class president, I don't

24   believe there's anything to concern yourself with at

25   this time. No one wants to hear you speak and no one

26   will ask you to.

27 JAMES: Two words for you, Olivia. Speech class.

28 OLIVA: Oh, speech class! So you're currently enrolled in

29   the most dreaded class that students are required to

30   take?

31 JAMES: Correct.

32 OLIVIA: Been there, done that.

33 JAMES: I hate that class. I even have dreams about it.

34   Nightmares!

35 OLIVIA: And what happens in your dreams?

1 JAMES: OK, so I'm standing in front of the entire
2   classroom ...
3 OLIVIA: Yes?
4 JAMES: In my underwear!
5 OLIVIA: In your underwear?
6 JAMES: Yes!
7 OLIVIA: Well, let me assure you that it's a common dream
8   for people who are fearful of public speaking. But
9   thank goodness, your dream will never come to pass.
10 JAMES: And how do you know, Miss Student Counselor?
11 OLIVIA: Because first of all, you'd have to get past the
12   front door of Crockett High wearing nothing but
13   your underwear. And that would never happen.
14   Security would take you down and haul you off in a
15   heartbeat.
16 JAMES: OK. Well, I have another fear.
17 OLIVIA: Go on.
18 JAMES: I have this fear that when I open my mouth,
19   nothing comes out. Like this. *(He opens his mouth to*
20   *demonstrate.)*
21 OLIVIA: Say something.
22 JAMES: What?
23 OLIVIA: Thank you.
24 JAMES: For what?
25 OLIVIA: You just spoke. Words did come out of your
26   mouth.
27 JAMES: But when I'm up there in front of everyone ...
28 OLIVIA: You'll get through it just fine.
29 JAMES: But I'm scared.
30 OLIVIA: Life can be scary at times.
31 JAMES: You know, you're not really helping.
32 OLIVIA: Gut it up. That's what I have to say.
33 JAMES: Gee, thanks. *(RACHEL enters. She is holding a*
34   *tissue and wiping her eyes.)*
35 OLIVIA: *(To RACHEL)* I'll be right with you. *(To JAMES)*

1   Was there anything else?
2 JAMES: Yeah. When will Mrs. Sweeney be back?
3 OLIVIA: On Monday.
4 JAMES: Great.
5 OLIVIA: Do you want to come back on Monday?
6 JAMES: No. It'll be too late.
7 OLIVIA: Too late?
8 JAMES: My speech is tomorrow.
9 OLIVIA: James ...
10 JAMES: Yes?
11 OLIVIA: You'll live. See you in fifth period.
12 JAMES: Thanks. Thanks a lot. *(Under his breath as he exits)*
13   Gut it up! You'll live! Some great advice she gave me!
14 OLIVIA: May I help you?
15 RACHEL: *(Upset)* I need to speak to Mrs. Sweeney.
16 OLIVIA: I'm sorry, but she's not here today. I'm filling in
17   for her. Would you like to talk?
18 RACHEL: *(Sniffling)* Yes. *(Sits down.)*
19 OLIVIA: What's your name?
20 RACHEL: Rachel.
21 OLIVIA: Rachel, how may I help you?
22 RACHEL: I don't think you can.
23 OLIVIA: Well, let's talk about it. What's wrong? Why are
24   you crying?
25 RACHEL: *(Crying)* My life is over!
26 OLIVIA: I wouldn't say that. You're still breathing, aren't
27   you?
28 RACHEL: Justin dumped me!
29 OLIVIA: Your boyfriend?
30 RACHEL: My ex-boyfriend!
31 OLIVIA: Ah, teen love.
32 RACHEL: I love him. I really, really love him. But what am
33   I supposed to do now? How am I supposed to go on?
34 OLIVIA: Yes, a broken heart is painful. But you will
35   survive this.

1   RACHEL: I don't see how.

2   ERIC: *(Rushes into the room.)* Mrs. Sweeney, my life is over.

3   *(To OLIVIA)* Who are you?

4   OLIVIA: Mrs. Sweeney is not here today. I'm filling in for

5   her. And as you can see, I'm with someone right now.

6   RACHEL: *(To ERIC)* My life is over, too.

7   ERIC: Really? Then can I join in on this counseling

8   session? Since both our lives are over?

9   OLIVIA: I don't think ...

10 RACHEL: It's fine with me.

11 ERIC: Thanks. *(Sits next to RACHEL.)* My girlfriend

12   dumped me. *(Snaps fingers.)* Like that! Nine months

13   of pure bliss, then, "I've met someone else, Eric. I'm

14   sorry. Please don't hate me." Well, you know what?

15 OLIVIA: You hate her?

16 ERIC: Yes! Yes, I do!

17 RACHEL: I don't hate Justin. *(Crying)* I love him.

18 ERIC: Oh, you'll get to the hate stage. Just wait. I skipped

19   the tears. *(Thinking)* But I wonder if that's healthy?

20   *(To OLIVIA)* Do you think I need to cry? You know, for

21   the healing process?

22 OLIVIA: Do you both want to hear what I think?

23 ERIC: Yes.

24 RACHEL: Yes.

25 OLIVIA: The best way to get over a broken heart is to jump

26   right into a new relationship.

27 RACHEL: Without giving yourself time to grieve?

28 ERIC: Or plan a good revenge?

29 OLIVIA: The best revenge is to move on. Quickly.

30 ERIC: You're right. Yeah!

31 RACHEL: And I don't really want Justin seeing me like

32   this. I want him to think I could care less that he

33   dumped me. *(Cries.)* But I do.

34 ERIC: *(To RACHEL)* Hey, do you want to have lunch

35   together?

1   RACHEL: You and me?

2   ERIC: Yes. And wouldn't it be great to enter the cafeteria

3   smiling ... laughing ... maybe even holding hands?

4   RACHEL: We're not allowed to hold hands in school.

5   ERIC: We are until we get caught. And if we get caught,

6   we'll say we forgot.

7   RACHEL: Oh! So your ex and my ex will see us. Together!

8   ERIC: Sounds like a good plan to me. Moving on with a

9   little slice of revenge.

10   RACHEL: I like it!

11   ERIC: *(Looks at his watch.)* And look at the time. The lunch

12   bell is about to ring. *(Stands, offering his hand.)* Shall

13   we?

14   RACHEL: *(Stands and takes his hand.)* We shall. *(They exit*

15   *holding hands. MRS. CARSON enters.)*

16   MRS. CARSON: Where's Mrs. Sweeney?

17   OLIVIA: Hi, Mrs. Carson. She's not here today. I'm filling

18   in for her.

19   MRS. CARSON: But you're a student.

20   OLIVIA: Yes ma'am.

21   MRS. CARSON: Well, you know what? I don't care. If I

22   don't talk to someone today, I'm going to lose my

23   mind!

24   OLIVIA: I thought Mrs. Sweeney only counseled students.

25   MRS. CARSON: Teachers as well. So, are you agreeable to

26   this?

27   OLIVIA: Sure. How may I help you, Mrs. Carson?

28   MRS. CARSON: *(Deep breath)* I'm just going to lay it out

29   there for you.

30   OLIVIA: OK.

31   MRS. CARSON: I hate my job.

32   OLIVIA: You hate teaching?

33   MRS. CARSON: Yes!

34   OLIVIA: I see ...

35   MRS. CARSON: I came into this profession with lots of

1	hope and enthusiasm. It was my dream job for as
2	long as I can remember. But then I got hired and
3	everything went downhill from there.
4	OLIVIA: What happened?
5	MRS. CARSON: What happened? I'll tell you what
6	happened! The students that I teach sucked all the
7	hope and enthusiasm out of me.
8	OLIVIA: The students?
9	MRS. CARSON: Yes! Those disrespectful and disruptive
10	jerks.
11	OLIVIA: Maybe you should send those students to me — I
12	mean Mrs. Sweeney — for counseling.
13	MRS. CARSON: An entire class? Can I send my entire class
14	here for counseling? Will you teach them to respect
15	their elders, make them do their homework, sit still,
16	be quiet, and listen while I teach? Can you do that?
17	Can you?!
18	OLIVIA: Well, I don't know if I can ...
19	MRS. CARSON: What I'd like to do is get a hold of one of
20	those disruptive brats and ... *(Choking motions)*
21	OLIVIA: Mrs. Carson! You can't do that.
22	MRS. CARSON: No? You're right, I can't! *(Points her finger*
23	*at OLIVIA.)* But *you* need to do something.
24	OLIVIA: Me?
25	MRS. CARSON: You're the counselor.
26	OLIVIA: If I might offer you some advice —
27	MRS. CARSON: *(Laughs.)* Advice! Oh, advice! As if that's
28	going to change the fact that I spend most of my day
29	dealing with behavioral problems instead of doing
30	what I was hired to do. Teach! But let me hear it. Let
31	me hear your so-called advice, Miss Student
32	Counselor.
33	OLIVIA: Well, first of all you must maintain order and
34	discipline in your classroom.
35	MRS. CARSON: *Duh!*

1   **OLIVIA: And keep your cool. Don't let the students know**
2   **that they are getting to you.**
3   **MRS. CARSON: You mean don't turn around and scream**
4   **and pull my hair when I've lost it? Like this?**
5   *(Demonstrates.)*
6   **OLIVIA: No! You can't do that. You're the teacher. Mrs.**
7   **Carson, repeat after me. I am the teacher.**
8   **MRS. CARSON:** *(Sarcastically)* **I am the teacher.**
9   **OLIVIA: And you will do as I say or suffer the**
10   **consequences.**
11   **MRS. CARSON:** *(Rolling her eyes)* **And you will do as I say or**
12   **suffer the consequences.**
13   **OLIVIA: First ...**
14   **MRS. CARSON:** *(Sarcastically)* **First ...**
15   **OLIVA: First offense will be a warning.**
16   **MRS. CARSON: Warning! Like that'll work. I warn all day**
17   **long. Sit down! Stop talking! Quit passing notes! Put**
18   **the candy up! Stop texting and calling friends during**
19   **class! But do they listen? Do they? No!**
20   **OLIVIA: Of course not. Second.**
21   **MRS. CARSON:** *(Sarcastically)* **Second?**
22   **OLIVIA: Zero.**
23   **MRS. CARSON: Zero?**
24   **OLIVIA: A big fat zero goes down in the grade book.**
25   **MRS. CARSON: Oh, I like that one. Big fat zero for you! You**
26   **want to fail my class? I don't care. Believe me, I do not**
27   **care. Fail, fail, fail if you want to, you stupid students.**
28   **Zero for bad behavior. Zero, zero, zero!** *(Gives an evil*
29   *laugh.)*
30   **OLIVIA: Third.**
31   **MRS. CARSON:** *(Getting into this)* **Third!**
32   **OLIVIA: Parent-teacher conference.**
33   **MRS. CARSON: But I don't like those.**
34   **OLIVA: You have to do it, Mrs. Carson. You have to let the**
35   **parents know that their child is being disruptive in**

1   your class.

2 MRS. CARSON: Can we skip the third consequence and

3   find something else?

4 OLIVIA: No. Parent-teacher conference. And fourth ...

5 MRS. CARSON: Fourth.

6 OLIVIA: You're out of here.

7 MRS. CARSON: You're out of here?

8 OLIVIA: Principal's office.

9 MRS. CARSON: Those students don't care about that.

10   They go down there, they come back. They go down

11   there, they come back. They go down there ...

12 OLIVIA: Stop! You need to let Mr. Fraser know that when

13   you send a student to his office, he better deal with it

14   in a serious matter. Because if their behavior doesn't

15   change, they will not be allowed back into your room.

16   Or else!

17 MRS. CARSON: Or else?

18 OLIVIA: You'll quit.

19 MRS. CARSON: That's not a bad idea.

20 OLIVIA: He can deal with your disruptive students or he

21   can find a replacement for you.

22 MRS. CARSON: I like that! I know Mr. Fraser can't stand to

23   lose another teacher. We're shorthanded as it is.

24 OLIVIA: Then that's the plan.

25 MRS. CARSON: Yes! And I like that plan. Thank you.

26   Thank you very much.

27 MR. FRASER: *(Rushes into the room.)* Mrs. Sweeney, I need

28   to talk to you. I hate my job. I hate the kids. And I

29   want to run away. *(Looks at OLIVIA.)* Oh, who are you?

30 MRS. CARSON: *(Stands.)* Student counselor. Good luck.

31   Oh, and Mr. Fraser?

32 MR. FRASER: Yes?

33 MRS. CARSON: When you're finished in here, I need to

34   have a little talk with you.

35 MR. FRASER: You do?

1   **MRS. CARSON: Yes. About you dealing with my disruptive**
2   **students. Or else!** *(She exits.)*
3   **OLIVIA: Mr. Fraser, try this one on for size. Straighten up**
4   **or it's detention for you!**
5   **MR. FRASER:** *(Whining)* **But I don't want to go to**
6   **detention. Can you send the principal to detention? I**
7   **try to be a good principal. I try to be a friend to the**
8   **students. Why do I have to go to detention?**
9   **OLIVIA: Not you!**
10   **MR. FRASER: Not me?**
11   **OLIVIA: The students!**
12   **MR. FRASER: Oh.**
13   **OLIVIA:** *(Shakes head.)* **You're going to be a tough one, Mr.**
14   **Fraser.**
15   **MR. FRASER: I am?**
16   **OLIVIA:** *(Slams fist into hand.)* **You've got to toughen up**
17   **and be mean! When those students are sent to your**
18   **office, you've got to be mean. Show them the fear of**
19   **God.**
20   **MR. FRASER:** *(Timidly)* **I'll try to be mean.**
21   **OLIVIA: Do it! Pretend I'm a disruptive, out-of-control**
22   **student who is in Mrs. Carson's class.**
23   **MR. FRASER: OK.**
24   **OLIVIA: And I show up in your office.**
25   **MR. FRASER: OK.**
26   **OLIVIA: Well? Scream at me or something.**
27   **MR. FRASER: I think we should talk.**
28   **OLIVIA: No! Say this, "Talking is over! It's time for action!"**
29   **MR. FRASER: But this is what I usually say. "Olivia, do you**
30   **think you can go back to the classroom and behave?"**
31   **OLIVIA:** *(Sweetly)* **Sure.**
32   **MR. FRASER: OK. Now scoot along back to class and don't**
33   **let me see you again.**
34   **OLIVIA: I'm back. Acted up again.**
35   **MR. FRASER: Why? Didn't you learn your lesson?**

1   **OLIVIA: No.**

2   **MR. FRASER: Well, that's not nice to disrupt the class.**

3   **Now can you go back and behave?**

4   **OLIVIA:** *(Sweetly)* **Sure.**

5   **MR. FRASER: OK. Run along, then.**

6   **OLIVIA: Mr. Fraser, you've got to get mean. Scream. Yell.**

7   **Slam your hand on the desk and holler at the**

8   **student.**

9   **MR. FRASER: Get mean?**

10   **OLIVIA: Yes! As mean as possible. So let me see it. So, here**

11   **I am, in your office for the third time for being**

12   **disruptive in Mrs. Carson's class. Now what are you**

13   **going to do?**

14   **MR. FRASER: Sit down and let's talk about it.**

15   **OLIVIA: No! Get mean, Mr. Fraser.**

16   **MR. FRASER:** *(Tries to yell and sound mean, but still comes*

17   *across nice.)* **Sit down and let's talk about it.**

18   **OLIVIA: Role reversal. I'm you and you're me.** *(They swap*

19   *places.)* **Oh, so you're in here again?**

20   **MR. FRASER: I'm sorry.**

21   **OLIVIA: Don't you sorry me, you disrespectful moron!**

22   *(Slams hand on desk.)* **Because you know what's going**

23   **to happen now?**

24   **MR. FRASER: No.**

25   **OLIVIA:** *(Screams.)* **Detention for the rest of the semester!**

26   **MR. FRASER: Detention?**

27   **OLIVIA: That's right. You get sent to my office, well, then,**

28   **you're going to deal with the consequences. And my**

29   **consequences aren't pretty. So how do you like them**

30   **apples?**

31   **MR. FRASER:** *(Puts his head in his hands and cries.)* **I'm**

32   **sorry.**

33   **OLIVIA: And do you think I care? Well, let me tell you**

34   **something. I don't care! You students think there's**

35   **nothing to it to be sent to the principal's office? Well,**

1   **think again. The tide has turned. Because the**
2   **students at Crockett High will fear me as I should be**
3   **feared.** *(Slams hand on desk.)* **And I will be feared.**
4   *(Pause)* **Mr. Fraser, do you see what I'm trying to show**
5   **you? Mr. Fraser? Mr. Fraser, why are you crying?**
6 MR. FRASER: *(Crying)* **Because I don't want to go to**
7   **detention.**

2. Show and Tell

CAST: (3M, 2F) TREVOR, MARK, ARIEL, MORGAN, ROBBY
PROPS: Vase with dirt inside, backpack
SETTING: School hallway

1   *(At rise, MARK is holding a vase.)*

2   **TREVOR: What's up with the vase?**

3   **MARK: It's for show and tell.**

4   **TREVOR: At our ages?**

5   **MARK: Mrs. Robinson wanted us to bring an item to class**

6   **that reflects something influential from our**

7   **childhood. A book, souvenir from a trip, family photo ...**

8   **TREVOR: What did you bring?**

9   **MARK: Uncle Lester.**

10   **TREVOR:** *(Looking around)* **Where is he?**

11   **MARK:** *(Holds up the vase.)* **In here. It's Uncle Lester's ashes.**

12   **TREVOR: You brought your cremated uncle to school?**

13   **MARK: Sure. Why not?**

14   **TREVOR: Is that allowed?**

15   **MARK: I don't know why not. It's just ashes.**

16   **TREVOR: Do your parents know you took Uncle Lester from**

17   **the mantel?**

18   **MARK: How did you know he was on the mantel?**

19   **TREVOR: Isn't that where everyone puts a person's ashes?**

20   **MARK: I guess. But no, I didn't tell my parents. They won't**

21   **even miss Uncle Lester. He'll be back on the mantel**

22   **before they have a chance to get home from work.**

23   **TREVOR: Can I see?**

24   **MARK: Sure.** *(Holds the vase for him to see inside.)*

25   **TREVOR:** *(To the vase)* **Hi, Uncle Lester. Sorry you died.** *(To*

26   *MARK)* **What happened?**

27   **MARK: Heart problems. He was only forty.**

28   **TREVOR: That's sad.** *(To the vase)* **Sorry you can't be here for**

29   **your nephew's show and tell assignment.**

1   MARK: Uncle Lester was awesome. And he spoiled me
2   rotten. Never had any of his own kids so he had all the
3   time in the world for me. Took me to amusement
4   parks, snow skiing, kayaking, hauled me around to
5   see national monuments and parks, took me fishing,
6   deer hunting ...
7   TREVOR: Wow. I wish I'd had an uncle like that.
8   MARK: And he gave the best presents ever. If there was
9   something I wanted, Uncle Lester made sure I got it.
10   *(Looks inside vase.)* I loved Uncle Lester.
11   TREVOR: He sounds awesome.
12   MARK: He was.
13   ARIEL: *(Enters.)* Hey, Trevor. Hey, Mark. What's in the
14   vase?
15   TREVOR: Mark brought his dead uncle to school.
16   ARIEL: *(Steps back.)* What?
17   TREVOR: Ariel, it's just his ashes.
18   ARIEL: Why would you do that? School is no place for a
19   dead person! Did he just die? Are you missing him so
20   much that you had to bring him with you?
21   MARK: Ariel, it's for show and tell. We're supposed to
22   bring something influential from our childhood so I
23   brought Uncle Lester.
24   ARIEL: Well, I hope you don't get into trouble for that.
25   MARK: Why would I?
26   ARIEL: Because you brought a dead person to school!
27   MARK: It's for show and tell.
28   ARIEL: Are you going to pass the vase around and let
29   everyone look inside?
30   TREVOR: He let me look.
31   ARIEL: Well, I don't want to see. Ewwww!
32   MARK: If people want to see, then they can see. But most
33   of all, it's a symbol of the respect and love I had for
34   Uncle Lester.
35   ARIEL: You should have brought a picture of him instead.

1   **MARK: I didn't want to bring a picture. That's what half**
2   **the people are doing. I wanted to be more creative. I**
3   **wanted to bring Uncle Lester with me.** *(Hugs the*
4   *vase.)* **I love him and miss him so much.**
5   **MORGAN:** *(Enters.)* **Hey, what's going on?** *(Points to the*
6   *vase.)* **What's that?**
7   **ARIEL: His Uncle Lester. Who's dead.**
8   **MORGAN: No way!**
9   **TREVOR: It's for show and tell.**
10   **MORGAN: Wow! And I just brought a photo of Grandma**
11   **Estelle.**
12   **MARK: See! Everyone will be bringing pictures.**
13   **TREVOR: Mark, you will be the most original. That's for**
14   **sure.**
15   **MORGAN: Can I see?**
16   **TREVOR: He let me see.**
17   **ARIEL: I don't want to see.**
18   **MARK: Sure you can, Morgan.**
19   **MORGAN:** *(Takes the vase from MARK and looks inside.*
20   *Gets teary.)* **What was his name?**
21   **MARK: Uncle Lester.**
22   **MORGAN: I'm so sorry! What happened?**
23   **MARK: Heart problems.**
24   **MORGAN: And you keep him close by? In your room?**
25   **MARK: Not in my room. Mom keeps Uncle Lester on the**
26   **mantel in the living room.**
27   **MORGAN: Of course. Poor Uncle Lester.** *(To the vase)* **I'm**
28   **so sorry you are no longer with us, Uncle Lester.**
29   **ARIEL: Morgan, why are you getting all teary? It's not like**
30   **you knew him.**
31   **MORGAN: No, I didn't know him, but it's sad seeing a**
32   **person like this.**
33   **TREVOR: It is sad.**
34   **MARK: He was my favorite uncle. And I still miss him.**
35   **MORGAN: I bet you do. Here, let me give Uncle Lester back**

1   **to you.** *(Her hand slips and she spills the ashes on the*
2   *floor.)* **Oh, Mark! I'm so sorry!** *(Everyone steps back.*
3   *They are silent, not knowing what to do.)*
4 **TREVOR: This is not good.**
5 **MARK:** *(Drops to his knees.)* **Uncle Lester!**
6 **ROBBY:** *(Entering, he walks on the ashes.)* **What did you**
7   **lose? A contact or something?**
8 **MARK: Robby, you're standing on Uncle Lester!**
9 **ROBBY: What?** *(Looks down.)* **I'm not standing on anyone.**
10   **Just some dirt, but that's no big deal.**
11 **ARIEL: Robby, move!**
12 **ROBBY: Why?**
13 **TREVOR: Just step back. OK?**
14 **ROBBY: Oh, are you afraid I stepped on your contact?**
15   *(Steps aside.)* **Sorry. Hope it's not on the bottom on my**
16   **shoe.** *(Lifts shoe.)* **Nope. Just a bunch of dirt.** *(They ALL*
17   *gasp.)*
18 **MARK: Robby, take off your shoes.**
19 **ROBBY: Why?**
20 **MARK: Just take them off. Now!** *(ROBBY pulls his shoes off.)*
21   **Do you see this on the bottom or your shoes?**
22 **ROBBY: Just some dirt.**
23 **MARK: This is Uncle Lester!**
24 **ROBBY: What are you talking about?**
25 **MARK:** *(Carefully dusting the ashes off his shoes and into*
26   *the vase.)* **Oh, Uncle Lester. I'm so sorry I let this**
27   **happen to you.**
28 **MORGAN: Robby, those are his uncle's ashes.**
29 **ARIEL: Yeah. He brought them to school for show and tell.**
30 **ROBBY: To school? Why?**
31 **TREVOR: To be original.**
32 **MORGAN: And I was looking inside the vase and when I**
33   **tried to hand it back to Mark, it slipped and ... oh, I'm**
34   **just so sorry!**
35 **ROBBY:** *(Jumps back.)* **I was stepping on a dead body?**

1   **TREVOR: His ashes.**

2   **ROBBY: Oh, man. Sorry!**

3   **MARK:** *(On his knees, sweeping up the ashes)* **What was I**

4   **thinking? I should have left Uncle Lester at home on**

5   **the mantel and brought a photo instead.**

6   **ARIEL: It was just an accident, Mark.**

7   **MORGAN:** *(Kneels.)* **I'll help you gather Uncle Lester.**

8   **ROBBY:** *(Kneels.)* **Me too.**

9   **TREVOR:** *(Kneels.)* **So will I.**

10   **MARK: Thanks, guys.**

11   **ARIEL: I would, but I can't. I just can't.**

12   **ROBBY: Maybe we should get a broom.**

13   **ARIEL: Or a dust buster.**

14   **MARK: No. Let's just carefully put him back into the vase.**

15   *(They put the ashes in the vase.)*

16   **ROBBY: You know, if you had to, you could throw a little**

17   **dirt in the vase and no one would know the**

18   **difference.**

19   **MARK: No! I would know the difference. And I would**

20   **never throw dirt in with Uncle Lester.**

21   **TREVOR:** *(Putting ashes in vase)* **Here we go. I think we got**

22   **most of it.**

23   **MARK: Don't you mean *most of him*?**

24   **ROBBY: And I think it's all off my shoes, too.** *(Claps shoes*

25   *together.)*

26   **MARK: What are you doing?!**

27   **ROBBY: Just making sure.**

28   **TREVOR:** *(Hands the vase to MARK.)* **Uncle Lester is back**

29   **where he belongs.**

30   **MARK: Thanks.** *(Stands with vase.)* **I sure hope we got all of**

31   **him.**

32   **ARIEL: I'm sure you did. Well, most of him, at least.**

33   **MORGAN: Again, I'm sorry, Mark.**

34   **MARK: It's OK, Morgan. I know it was an accident.** *(To the*

35   *vase)* **Come on, Uncle Lester, I'm taking you home**

1   where you belong. *(Exits.)*
2   ROBBY: Look. There's still a little on the floor. Hey, Mark!
3   TREVOR: No! Don't tell him. He'll just get upset. And in the
4   long run it's not really going to matter.
5   MORGAN: Poor Uncle Lester.
6   TREVOR: *(Shuffles feet.)* We'll just spread the ashes
7   around on the floor. And who will ever know?
8   ARIEL: I will. Ewwww!
9   MARK: *(Enters.)* Hey, I'm back. I forgot my backpack. And
10   my house key is in it. *(He grabs his backpack, then*
11   *trips, spilling the ashes on the floor. Everyone is silent.)*
12   Uncle Lester!
13   TREVOR: I'll get a broom. *(Exits.)*
14   MORGAN: I'll get a dustpan. *(Exits.)*
15   ARIEL: I'm sorry, but I just can't deal with this. *(Exits.)*
16   ROBBY: *(Looks at his watch.)* Lunchtime. *(Exits.)*
17   MARK: *(Scooping up the ashes)* Oh, Uncle Lester!

3. Bubble Wrap Obsession

CAST: (3F) TAYLOR, SHELBY, ERIN
PROPS: Plastic bubble wrap, boxes with glassware or
  breakables wrapped in the plastic bubble wrap
SETTING: Gift shop

1   *(At rise, SHELBY is holding bubble wrap and popping the*
2   *bubbles.)*
3   **TAYLOR: Shelby, stop.**
4   **SHELBY: I can't. It's addicting.**
5   **TAYLOR: It's getting on my nerves.**
6   **SHELBY: You should try it, Taylor.**
7   **TAYLOR: We don't have time to play with bubble wrap. We**
8   **need to unpack these boxes so we can go home.**
9   **ERIN:** *(Enters carrying a box.)* **Here's the last box off the**
10   **truck.** *(Kneels down.)* **Shelby, why are you just standing**
11   **there?**
12 **TAYLOR: She's obsessed with bubble wrap.**
13 **ERIN: Shelby, Mr. Rodriguez said we have to unpack the**
14   **merchandise before we can go home. And I want to go**
15   **home.**
16 **TAYLOR: I reminded her. But she won't stop.**
17 **SHELBY: Give me a minute.** *(Pops the bubbles.)* **I like feeling**
18   **the bubble between my fingers. And I love the feeling**
19   **of power when I pop them.** *(Pops bubble.)*
20 **ERIN: And I like it when we work together as a team and**
21   **finish our work so we can all go home.**
22 **TAYLOR: Because at this rate, you're going to make our part-**
23   **time job turn into a full-time job.**
24 **SHELBY:** *(Popping)* **You should try it.**
25 **TAYLOR: Shelby, come on.**
26 **ERIN: Please come help us.**
27 **SHELBY:** *(Popping)* **But it's fun.**
28 **TAYLOR:** *(Stands, goes to SHELBY, and snatches the bubble*

1 *wrap from her hands.)* **Stop it! Now you're in charge of**
2 **unpacking that box. Got it? Got it!** *(Returns to*
3 *unpacking.)*
4 **ERIN: And as we all know, the gift shop needs gifts to put**
5 **on the shelves. And when the truck comes in with**
6 **merchandise on Thursdays, it's our job to unload and**
7 **unpack.** *(Looks at SHELBY.)* **As a team. Equal work.**
8 **Equal pay.**
9 **SHELBY:** *(Picks up another piece of bubble wrap and starts*
10 *popping.)* **I just can't stop!**
11 **ERIN: Shelby!** *(To TAYLOR)* **We're going to be here all**
12 **night.**
13 **TAYLOR: Unless we can figure out a way to make her stop.**
14 **Hey, Shelby, I heard that bubble wrap causes cancer.**
15 **SHELBY:** *(Popping)* **Everything causes cancer.**
16 **ERIN: It'll give you tendonitis in your thumb.**
17 **SHELBY: I don't care.**
18 **TAYLOR: You'll turn into an obsessive-compulsive person.**
19 **ERIN:** *(To TAYLOR)* **I think she already has.**
20 **TAYLOR: And your life will pass you by as you spend your**
21 **days popping plastic air bubbles. What a waste.**
22 **ERIN: All day and all night.**
23 **TAYLOR: No life outside popping bubbles.**
24 **ERIN: Your parents will forget who you are.**
25 **TAYLOR: Your friends will stop asking you to hang out.**
26 **ERIN: Those fun college years will be spent all alone.**
27 **TAYLOR: Popping bubbles.**
28 **ERIN: All day and all night.**
29 **TAYLOR: Then eventually this obsessive-compulsive**
30 **disorder will require counseling.**
31 **ERIN: And medications.**
32 **TAYLOR: And that can get very expensive. The doctor**
33 **visits, prescriptions ...**
34 **ERIN: And then you're looking at your part-time job**
35 **turning into a full-time job just to pay for your**

1   popping disorder.

2   TAYLOR: Such a sad and lonely life it will be.

3   SHELBY: *(Happily popping away)* I love this! The power.

4   The control. Pop. Pop. Pop!

5   TAYLOR: *(To ERIN)* This isn't working.

6   ERIN: *(Stands and goes to SHELBY and grabs the bubble*

7   *wrap.)* **Stop it!** *(She pops a bubble, smiles, then pops*

8   *another and now can't stop.)*

9   SHELBY: Fun, isn't it? *(Picks up another piece of bubble*

10   *wrap and begins popping alongside ERIN.)*

11   TAYLOR: Erin! Not you, too.

12   ERIN: It is fun. And it does give you a powerful feeling

13   when you pop the little suckers. *(Pops.)* Take that!

14   And that!

15   TAYLOR: Erin! Shelby! Come on. We need to unpack these

16   boxes.

17   ERIN: *(To SHELBY)* Have you ever finished popping an

18   entire piece of plastic wrap?

19   SHELBY: Yes. That's the goal every time.

20   ERIN: Yes! I want to pop every bubble in this piece of

21   plastic.

22   SHELBY: Then you're the winner.

23   TAYLOR: Of what? The bubble wrap game?

24   ERIN: *(Popping)* I do like the power.

25   SHELBY: The power is within you.

26   ERIN: *(Popping)* Die! Die! Die!

27   SHELBY: Maybe people who have controlling

28   personalities enjoy this. *(Pops.)* I am in control. Not

29   you.

30   ERIN: Or people who need to release their pent up

31   frustrations. *(Pops.)* Take that. And that. And here's

32   to you, differential equations. *(Pops.)* I hate you. I

33   hate you. I hate you.

34   TAYLOR: And I hate doing all this work by myself. You two

35   playing while I'm working. It's not fair!

1   ERIN: Come try it, Taylor.

2   TAYLOR: No! But why don't you two come help me unpack

3   these boxes?

4   ERIN: *(Ignoring her)* I love popping.

5   SHELBY: Me too.

6   ERIN: Pop. Pop. Pop!

7   SHELBY: Pop. Pop. Pop!

8   TAYLOR: Well then, I guess I need to have a little talk with

9   Mr. Rodriguez. You know, *our boss.* "Mr. Rodriguez,

10   they left me to do all the work by myself. That's right!

11   They just sat around and popped plastic bubbles

12   while I slaved away. And by the way, can I have a

13   raise? I can? Thank you. And one more thing. Can you

14   fire Shelby and Erin? You can? Thank you!"

15   ERIN: Pop. Pop. Pop.

16   SHELBY: Pop. Pop. Pop.

17   TAYLOR: "And Mr. Rodriguez, I'll need two new co-

18   workers. Because it's impossible to unpack all the

19   merchandise by yourself while your coworkers are

20   doing this. *(Picks up some bubble wrap and pops it. In*

21   *a hateful tone)* Pop. Pop. Pop.

22   ERIN: *(Popping)* I love it.

23   SHELBY: Me, too.

24   TAYLOR: Pop. Pop. Pop.

25   SHELBY: Fun isn't it, Taylor?

26   TAYLOR: *(Popping)* I don't know what happened, but now

27   I can't stop.

28   ERIN: Addicting, isn't it?

29   TAYLOR: Why can't I stop?

30   SHELBY: I can't stop.

31   ERIN: Me neither.

32   TAYLOR: *(Smiles.)* But I love it. This is fun! Pop. Pop. Pop!

4. My Dog Ate My Homework

CAST: (3M) MR. HILL, ADAM, RASHAUN
PROPS: Grade book, tray to turn in homework assignments
SETTING: Classroom

1 *(At rise, ADAM approaches MR. HILL, who is sitting*
2 *behind his desk.)*
3 **MR. HILL:** *(Writing in a grade book, not looking up)* **Yes?**
4 **ADAM: Mr. Hill, about my homework ...**
5 **MR. HILL: In the tray please.**
6 **ADAM: Well, there's a problem.**
7 **MR. HILL: A problem? You mean you didn't understand how**
8   **to determine the midpoint of a line segment? The**
9   **midpoint formula is simple. To determine the**
10   **midpoint, you need to know the x and y coordinates of**
11   **your two points. Two x coordinates and two y**
12   **coordinates. When you have these values the process is**
13   **easy. Homework in the tray, please. And I hope you**
14   **showed your work. Because you know what happens**
15   **when you don't. Zero!**
16 **ADAM: Mr. Hill, it's not that I didn't understand. I mean, I**
17   **kind of understood. Not really, but I did the best I could**
18   **with it. And I did my homework, but there's a problem**
19   **with my homework.**
20 **MR. HILL: Adam, place your homework in the tray and quit**
21   **babbling and wasting my time.**
22 **ADAM: But I can't place it in the tray because I don't have it**
23   **with me.**
24 **MR. HILL:** *(Shuts grade book.)* **Oh! So this is where you are**
25   **going to try to explain to me why you don't have your**
26   **homework to turn in. Every day. So many excuses and**
27   **I've heard them all. But I'm listening. Let's hear it.**
28 **ADAM: Mr. Hill, my dog ate my homework.**
29 **MR. HILL: Your dog ate your homework?**

1   ADAM: Yes sir.

2   MR. HILL: *(Laughs.)* How lame is that!

3   ADAM: But it's true.

4   MR. HILL: Talk about an unoriginal excuse! *(Laughs and*

5   *opens grade book.)* Where are you? Oh here you are.

6   Adam Webber. *(Writing)* Zero! Fourth one in six

7   weeks. Not looking good for you, Mr. Webber.

8   ADAM: But Mr. Hill, I did my homework. All of it. And I

9   showed my work. But my dog ate my homework.

10   Really. It's true.

11 MR. HILL: *(Mocking)* "Really! It's true!" Mr. Webber, can't

12   you be more creative? How about this one? My little

13   brother spilled cherry Kool-Aid on my homework.

14 ADAM: But I don't have a little brother.

15 MR. HILL: Well, it would've sounded more believable. And

16   it possibly would have gotten you an extension on

17   your homework assignment. But my dog ate my

18   homework? Ha! Zero for you. And you know what?

19   Maybe I should give you two zeros. One for not

20   turning in your homework and one for lying.

21 ADAM: But I'm not lying Mr. Hill.

22 MR. HILL: Liar, liar, pants on fire.

23 ADAM: Mr. Hill!

24 MR. HILL: Wanna hear a good one?

25 ADAM: A joke?

26 MR. HILL: No, an excuse. I hear them all the time. Every

27   day.

28 ADAM: Uh ... sure.

29 MR. HILL: "The wind blew it out of my hands!" *(Waves.)*

30   Good-bye! Or this one sounds believable. "Someone

31   stole it!" Then I say, "Then do it again!" Or how about

32   this one? "Mr. Hill, I was sick last night. But thank

33   God I made a miraculous recovery this morning." Or

34   how about these? "I left it in the car. I left it on the

35   bus. I left it at the track field. Dropped it in the

1   swimming pool. A tornado picked it up and

2   destroyed it. My brother ate it. My hamster ate it. My

3   garbage disposal ate it." But my dog ate it? Please!

4 ADAM: But it's true.

5 MR. HILL: "But it's true!" Please. Want to hear an excuse

6   the girls always give me?

7 ADAM: I guess.

8 MR. HILL: *(Whimpering)* "I can't find it!" *(Begins to cry.)* "I

9   looked everywhere for it and I don't know what

10   happened to it! *(Cries louder.)* Please, Mr. Hill, give

11   me the chance to do it again! Please!" *(Stops crying*

12   *and looks at ADAM.)* Maybe you should have cried.

13 ADAM: I can if it would help.

14 MR. HILL: It won't.

15 ADAM: Mr. Hill, what do I have to do to make you believe

16   me?

17 MR. HILL: Well, a picture of your homework hanging out

18   of your dog's mouth would help. Do you have that?

19 ADAM: No sir.

20 MR. HILL: A witness?

21 ADAM: My cat. Sassy saw the whole thing. I'd finished my

22   homework and left it on the kitchen table. When I

23   went to the refrigerator for a snack, I guess Sassy,

24   who was sleeping on the table, stretched her legs and

25   pushed my homework onto the floor. So then I

26   returned to the table to eat my sandwich. Well, I

27   didn't know that my homework had fallen onto the

28   floor. And anyway, Jack, my dog, started begging for

29   some of my sandwich. I know I shouldn't feed him

30   table food, but we do it all the time. So, I tore off a

31   piece of my sandwich and tossed it to him. But

32   instead of landing in Jack's mouth, it landed on my

33   homework. And Jack, being the pig that he is,

34   gobbled up the sandwich along with my homework.

35   Like this. *(Demonstrates.)*

1 MR. HILL: So you're telling me that your dog Jack ate
2   himself a homework sandwich?
3 ADAM: Yes sir.
4 MR. HILL: At least that story is more creative. "I fed my
5   dog a homework sandwich." I like it.
6 ADAM: You like it?
7 MR. HILL: Yes. I love good excuses. And you know ... if you
8   could do one more thing I might believe you and feel
9   sorry for you.
10 ADAM: What's that?
11 MR. HILL: Cry.
12 ADAM: Cry? You want me to cry?
13 MR. HILL: Yes. That's what gets to me every time.
14 ADAM: *(After a short pause, he begins to cry.)* Oh, Mr. Hill! I
15   don't know how it happened. My sandwich fell on my
16   homework and my dog gobbled it all up. He's a pig,
17   Mr. Hill. I think I'm going to change Jack's name to
18   Pig. He eats everything in sight! Sandwiches,
19   homework assignments, bars of soap, dirty socks ...
20   Oh, Mr. Hill ... *(Cries loudly.)*
21 MR. HILL: *(Dryly)* You have until tomorrow to turn in your
22   assignment.
23 ADAM: *(Stops crying.)* I do?
24 MR. HILL: You do. Now go on.
25 ADAM: Thank you, Mr. Hill. Thank you! Thank you, thank
26   you, thank you!
27 MR. HILL: All right, all right, that's enough.
28 ADAM: I'll turn my homework in first thing tomorrow.
29   Thank you! Thank you, thank you, thank you. *(He
30   exits and approaches RASHAUN who is waiting outside
31   the classroom.)*
32 MR. HILL: *(Under his breath)* Thank you, thank you, thank
33   you.
34 RASHAUN: Did it work?
35 ADAM: Yes, but it was tough. I should've gone with my first

1   instinct. The hamster ate my homework.
2   **RASHAUN:** Why?
3   **ADAM:** Mr. Hill likes creative excuses. The more creative
4   the better.
5   **RASHAUN:** Thanks for the tip, because I'm going in there
6   next. I better come up with something good.
7   **ADAM:** Yes, you should. And you need something
8   brilliant. Maybe this, "I lost my homework when I
9   was parachuting out of an airplane."
10 **RASHAUN:** Or how about this? "A relative died and I had
11   to attend an emergency funeral."
12 **ADAM:** Yeah, that's good. But you need to be sure and add
13   one more thing.
14 **RASHUAN:** What's that?
15 **ADAM:** Crying. That gets to Mr. Hill every time.
16 **RASHAUN:** I can do that. *(Cries.)* Mr. Hill ... a relative
17   died ...
18 **ADAM:** That's good, Rashaun. Good luck.
19 **RASHAUN:** Thanks. *(Approaches MR. HILL.)* Mr. Hill ...
20 **MR. HILL:** *(Writing in his grade book, not looking up)*
21   Homework in the tray, please.
22 **RASHAUN:** Mr. Hill, I need to talk to you about my
23   homework. *(Cries.)* A relative died and I had to attend
24   an emergency funeral.
25 **MR. HILL:** A relative died?
26 **RASHAUN:** Yes sir.
27 **MR. HILL:** Emergency funeral?
28 **RASHAUN:** Yes sir.
29 **MR. HILL:** Ha! *(Opens grade book.)* Zero!
30 **RASHAUN:** *(Dramatically falls to the ground, begging and
31   crying.)* Mr. Hill, you have to believe me!
32 **MR. HILL:** *(Smiles.)* Now it's getting good. Go on.
33 **RASHAUN:** *(Crying, wailing, looking heavenward, and
34   raising his hands)* Oh, he's gone! Here today, gone
35   tomorrow. A life that ended so soon. How will we go

1   **on? How will life ever be the same? His passing was so**
2   **painful. So painful I could not concentrate on earthly**
3   **matters such as homework. Homework is so trivial**
4   **compared to death. Oh ... oh ... oh ... the pain of his**
5   **loss.** *(Falls over in agony, crying.)* **May you rest in**
6   **peace.**
7 **MR. HILL: Rashaun.**
8 **RASHUAN:** *(Still bent over, crying)* **Yes sir?**
9 **MR. HILL: Turn in your homework assignment by**
10   **tomorrow.**
11 **RASHUAN:** *(Looks up, smiling.)* **Really?**
12 **MR. HILL: Yes. Now, go on.**
13 **RASHAUN:** *(Stands.)* **Thank you, Mr. Hill! Thank you!**
14   *(Exits.)* **Yes!** *(He finds ADAM, nods, and they high-five.)*

5. A Fine Line between Love and Hate

CAST: (2M, 2F) ADRIAN, WHITNEY, KATIE, CHRIS
SETTING: Outside of school

1   *(At rise, ADRIAN and WHITNEY are Center Stage facing*
2   *one another. KATIE stands at stage right waiting for*
3   *WHITNEY while CHRIS stands at stage left waiting for*
4   *ADRIAN.)*
5   **ADRIAN: So it's settled?**
6   **WHITNEY: It's settled.**
7   **ADRIAN: We're over?**
8   **WHITNEY: We're over.**
9   **ADRIAN:** *(Offers his hand.)* **Friends?**
10 **WHITNEY:** *(Takes his hand.)* **Friends.** *(ADRIAN leaves and*
11   *goes to CHRIS. WHITNEY leaves and goes to KATIE. Each*
12   *group takes turns speaking.)*
13 **WHITNEY:** *(To KATIE)* **Well, we worked it out.**
14 **KATIE: What happened?**
15 **WHITNEY: Adrian and I agreed to break up and remain**
16   **friends.**
17 **KATIE: You two broke up?** *(WHITNEY nods.)*
18 **ADRIAN:** *(To CHRIS)* **I thought it was for the best. An easy**
19   **split. No fighting. No forcing it to work. Just go our**
20   **separate ways and stay friends.**
21 **CHRIS: I've never known a girl who could be friends with**
22   **you after a breakup.**
23 **ADRIAN: Well, Whitney and I are no ordinary couple. I'd say**
24   **we're more mature and levelheaded than most teens.**
25 **CHRIS: She dumped you, didn't she?**
26 **ADRIAN: No! I told you it was a mutual decision.**
27 **CHRIS: Man, I wish I could have a mutual decision with a**
28   **girl for once. They always dump me before I see it**
29   **coming. One day we're in love, then the next day she's**

1   feeling smothered, or tied down, or too young for a
2   serious relationship. Then she hates my guts and
3   never speaks to me again. Go figure.
4 ADRIAN: No need for dramatics. We faced the facts. It's
5   over. Time to move on and go our separate ways.
6 CHRIS: Friends. Really?
7 ADRIAN: Absolutely. We tried to make it work. We
8   couldn't. So there's no point in being miserable.
9 CHRIS: You two were never miserable.
10 ADRIAN: Things change.
11 KATIE: But you guys have been together for a year. And
12   you even said you hoped it would last forever.
13 WHITNEY: I changed my mind.
14 KATIE: Why? What happened?
15 WHITNEY: It just became the same ole, same ole ... You
16   know?
17 KATIE: You're bored with Adrian?
18 WHITNEY: And he's bored with me. We know absolutely
19   everything about each other. Like I know how he
20   chomps his gum uncontrollably when he's got a lot
21   on his mind. Or how he hums the *Gilligan's Island*
22   tune when he's sitting in my living room waiting for
23   me to get ready for a date. Or how he nervously bites
24   his cuticles before a track meet or any major test.
25 KATIE: But familiarity is comfortable. Don't you think?
26 WHITNEY: I think it's become what I said. Same ole, same
27   ole. We're bored and tired of each other.
28 KATIE: And you're going to remain friends?
29 WHITNEY: Absolutely.
30 KATIE: I couldn't do it. I end up hating every guy I've ever
31   dated. Don't ask me why, but it just happens. And I
32   think it happens with most people.
33 WHITNEY: Well, I don't hate Adrian.
34 ADRIAN: I don't hate Whitney.
35 CHRIS: No?

1 ADRIAN: No. The way I see it, it's time to move on.
2   **Freedom.** *(Looks around and smiles.)* **Yeah, freedom.**
3   **Hello, girls. Here I am!**
4 CHRIS: So no bad feelings about the breakup?
5 ADRIAN: None at all.
6 CHRIS: And no regrets?
7 ADRIAN: No regrets at all. I feel good about my decision.
8 CHRIS: To part and remain friends?
9 ADRIAN: Yes.
10 CHRIS: But how are you going to feel when Whitney
11   hooks up with another guy?
12 ADRIAN: What?
13 KATIE: So it won't bother you if Adrian starts dating other
14   girls?
15 WHITNEY: Other girls?
16 KATIE: Like Megan. Or Alyssa. They both think Adrian is
17   cute and I don't think it'll take long before –
18 WHITNEY: He's not going to date other girls.
19 ADRIAN: It's going to take her months, maybe years to get
20   over me.
21 CHRIS: Nah. I'd say a couple days at the most. Girls don't
22   like to be alone. It's good for their ego to have guys
23   chase them. She'll move on. And quickly, I might add.
24 ADRIAN: No, I'm telling you, Whitney is not interested in
25   any other guys. Not after what we had together.
26 CHRIS: Parker likes her. At least that's what he told me.
27 ADRIAN: What? Parker has a thing for Whitney? *My*
28   *girlfriend?*
29 CHRIS: Uh ... your ex-girlfriend.
30 WHITNEY: Megan and Alyssa better just keep their hands
31   off my guy!
32 KATIE: Your guy?
33 WHITNEY: My ex-boyfriend ... whatever!
34 CHRIS: Hey, it's bound to happen. You move on, she
35   moves on, you move on ...

1 **ADRIAN:** You know, it was fine for me to move on. But her
2   moving on ... ?
3 **CHRIS:** You'll get used to it.
4 **KATIE:** Well, at least the two of you will remain friends.
5 **WHITNEY:** Friends while he slobbers all over Megan or
6   Alyssa? I don't think so!
7 **CHRIS:** Parker will be thrilled to hear the news. Whitney
8   is free. Of course you are too.
9 **ADRIAN:** I don't think I thought this through.
10 **CHRIS:** Obviously.
11 **ADRIAN:** This is not going to work.
12 **CHRIS:** But you said the two of you could remain friends.
13 **ADRIAN:** Friends! With her dating Parker? I don't think
14   so.
15 **KATIE:** So are you rethinking your breakup with Adrian?
16 **WHITNEY:** Do you think that's why he broke up with me?
17   So he could date Megan or Alyssa?
18 **KATIE:** I thought you said the breakup was mutual.
19 **WHITNEY:** It was, but it's not now.
20 **ADRIAN:** So she's going to start dating Parker? The
21   quarterback? Isn't that just fine and dandy.
22 **CHRIS:** Adrian, he hasn't asked her out. Yet. But as soon as
23   he hears ... He'll be running toward the goal. Your ex-
24   girlfriend, Whitney.
25 **ADRIAN:** And you know what? I'm going to tackle that jerk
26   before he has the chance to ask her out.
27 **CHRIS:** Whoa! You can't do that. You two broke up. Mutual
28   decision. Remaining friends. Remember?
29 **ADRIAN:** You know what? I'm starting to hate Whitney!
30 **CHRIS:** *(As if he knew it would happen)* **Uh-huh.** *(Looks at*
31   *his watch.)* **And only within a few minutes of the**
32   **breakup. That was fast.**
33 **ADRIAN:** That's right. I hate her! If she wants to date Mr.
34   Quarterback ... well, good luck with that.
35 **WHITNEY:** I'm beginning to hate Adrian.

1 KATIE: *(As if she knew it would happen)* **Uh-huh.**

2 WHITNEY: **He's bored with me? Well I'm mega bored with**
3   **him. Those stupid songs he hums. The *Jeopardy* song**
4   **really gets on my nerves. I thought if he hummed**
5   **that song one more time, I might ...** *(Shakes head.)*

6 ADRIAN: **I bet Whitney and her new quarterback**
7   **boyfriend won't last two weeks.**

8 CHRIS: **You guys lasted a year. They could last awhile.**
9   **Maybe.**

10 ADRIAN: **I don't know when I ever loathed someone so**
11   **much.**

12 WHITNEY: **I bet Megan and Alyssa will detest his little**
13   **humming.**

14 KATIE: **Alyssa said he hummed her the "Happy Birthday"**
15   **song during math class last week. She said he was so**
16   **adorable.**

17 WHITNEY: **Adorable? She said he was adorable?**

18 KATIE: **That's what she said.**

19 WHITNEY: **Adrian is not adorable! He's this ...** *(Makes*
20   *noises, such as "Uuuuh ... Ooooh ... " unable to find the*
21   *right words.)*

22 KATIE: **But you used to think he was adorable. And sweet**
23   **and cute and —**

24 WHITNEY: **My, how things change, don't they? I've never**
25   **disliked someone so much in my entire life. Katie, I**
26   **absolutely cannot stand Adrian. I never want to be in**
27   **the same room with him, cross his path, and for sure**
28   **look at his horrible face again!**

29 ADRIAN: **She can just ...** *Oh!*

30 WHITNEY: **And may his memory be deleted from my**
31   **mind!** *Oh!*

32 CHRIS: **Maybe the two of you need to talk.**

33 ADRIAN: **Talk to her?**

34 KATIE: **Maybe breaking up wasn't the best thing to do.**

35 WHITNEY: **Of course it was! It was the best thing I've ever**

1   done in my life.

2 **CHRIS: Give it a second chance.**

3 **ADRIAN: A second chance?**

4 **CHRIS: I think you still love Whitney.**

5 **ADRIAN: No I don't.**

6 **KATIE: I think you still love Adrian.**

7 **WHITNEY: No I don't.**

8 **CHRIS: Maybe you should tell her you miss her.**

9 **ADRIAN: After five minutes of breaking up?**

10 **CHRIS: Tell her you made a mistake.**

11 **ADRIAN: But what if she doesn't think she made a**
12   **mistake?**

13 **CHRIS: Can't know till you try.**

14 **KATIE: Admit it, Whitney. You still have feelings for**
15   **Adrian.**

16 **WHITNEY: Well, it doesn't matter because we broke up.**

17 **KATIE: Maybe you should tell him you miss him.**

18 **WHITNEY: Why? He doesn't miss me.**

19 **KATIE: I bet he does.**

20 **WHITNEY: You think?**

21 **CHRIS: Walk over there and talk to her. Be a man.**

22 **ADRIAN: What am I supposed to say?**

23 **CHRIS: You'll figure it out when you see her. Go!** *(ADRIAN*
24   *moves to Center Stage, but hesitates to go to WHITNEY.)*

25 **KATIE: Look! Adrian is standing over there all alone. Go**
26   **talk to him.**

27 **WHITNEY: And say what?**

28 **KATIE: Say hi! You said the two of you were going to**
29   **remain friends. Friends say hi.**

30 **WHITNEY:** *(Deep breath)* **OK.** *(She goes to ADRIAN. There is*
31   *a long pause.)*

32 **ADRIAN:** *(Quickly)* **I miss you.**

33 **WHITNEY: You do?**

34 **ADRIAN: I do.**

35 **WHITNEY: I miss you too.**

1 **ADRIAN: You do?**

2 **WHITNEY: I do.**

3 **ADRIAN: Let's not break up.**

4 **WHITNEY: I don't want to.**

5 **ADRIAN: Me neither.** *(ADRIAN takes her hand. As they are*

6 *exiting, he begins humming a song, such as the*

7 Jeopardy *theme song.)*

6. You Break, You Pay

CAST: (1M, 4F) JULIA, LYDIA, MACK, SASHA, MARGIE
PROPS: Broken plate, purse
SETTING: China store

1   *(At rise, LYDIA is standing over a broken plate. JULIA*
2   *enters and sees the plate on the floor.)*
3   **JULIA:** *(Pointing to the plate)* **Did you do this?**
4   **LYDIA: I'm sorry. My purse barely touched the table and it**
5   **fell over.**
6   **JULIA: You break, you pay.**
7   **LYDIA: But ...**
8   **JULIA: That dinner plate costs one hundred, forty-nine**
9   **dollars and ninety-eight cents.**
10 **LYDIA: For one plate?**
11 **JULIA:** *(Rudely)* **That, my dear, is an Alsager Rose dinner**
12   **plate.**
13 **LYDIA: But I was just browsing and my purse barely**
14   **touched the table and ... and I don't have one hundred,**
15   **forty-nine dollars and ninety-eight cents.**
16 **JULIA: Then I will call security.**
17 **LYDIA: For breaking a plate?**
18 **JULIA: It's a crime in my china store. See our sign over**
19   **there? You break, you pay. And did you read the fine**
20   **print?**
21 **LYDIA: No.** *(Squinting her eyes)* **It's too small to read.**
22 **JULIA: It says, "Once broken, considered sold. And failure to**
23   **do so will result in a crime punishable by**
24   **imprisonment."** *(Holds out her hand.)* **I accept cash and**
25   **credit cards.**
26 **LYDIA: But I don't have that kind of money to pay for the**
27   **plate. But I could write you an I-O-U.**
28 **JULIA: Unacceptable.**
29 **LYDIA: But if I don't have the money ...**

1 JULIA: *(Hollers.)* **Security! Security!**

2 LYDIA: **Wait! What are you doing?**

3 JULIA: **Calling security before you get away.**

4 LYDIA: **Wait! Look, I'll come back and pay you later. When**

5   **I have the money.**

6 JULIA: **Oh, you're not going anywhere, Missy! No, I take**

7   **that back. You are going somewhere. Jail.** *(Hollers.)*

8   **Security.**

9 LYDIA: **Jail? For a broken dinner plate?**

10 JULIA: **Perhaps you have a family member to call?**

11   **Someone to bring you the money so you won't be**

12   **hauled off in handcuffs.**

13 LYDIA: **Are you serious? Jail? Over a plate?**

14 JULIA: **I don't lie.** *(MACK, the security guard enters. JULIA*

15   *points to the floor.)* **Right here. Broken plate. It's an**

16   **Alsager Rose.** *(Looks at LYDIA as she speaks.)* **A very**

17   **expensive piece of fine china.**

18 MACK: **I'll get the broom, Miss Julia.** *(He starts off.)*

19 JULIA: **Mack! Not the broom. The handcuffs.**

20 LYDIA: **Look, Mr. Security Guard, it was an accident. I**

21   **didn't do it on purpose. See, I turned and my purse**

22   **barely touched the table. And then the plate fell and**

23   **... it was an accident. I swear.**

24 JULIA: **The Alsager Rose dinner plate. Worth one**

25   **hundred, forty-nine dollars and ninety-eight cents.**

26 LYDIA: **But I don't have one hundred, forty-nine dollars**

27   **and ninety-eight cents.**

28 JULIA: **Mack, lock her up and throw away the key until she**

29   **pays.**

30 LYDIA: **I'll write an I-O-U.**

31 JULIA: **Handcuff her, Mack.**

32 MACK: **Ma'am, I'm sorry, but you're going to have to come**

33   **with me.**

34 LYDIA: **You're arresting me?**

35 MACK: **Come with me, please.**

1   **LYDIA: Noooo!**

2   **SASHA:** *(Enters.)* **Hi, Lydia. What's going on? Are you in**

3   **some kind of trouble here?**

4   **JULIA: A friend has come to save you from imprisonment.**

5   *(To SASHA)* **Can you loan her one hundred, forty-nine**

6   **dollars and ninety-eight cents?**

7   **SASHA: What's going on here? What happened?**

8   **LYDIA: I broke a plate and they want to take me to jail.**

9   **JULIA: An Alsager Rose dinner plate.**

10 **LYDIA: It was an accident! Sasha, do you have some money**

11   **I can borrow? I'll pay you back.**

12 **SASHA: I have twenty dollars.**

13 **JULIA: Credit cards are accepted.**

14 **SASHA: I don't own a credit card. Don't believe in them.**

15 **MACK: Ma'am, if you would please come with me.** *(He*

16   *escorts LYDIA off.)*

17 **LYDIA:** *(As she is leaving)* **Sasha, tell my friends and family**

18   **I love them. Tell them I need an attorney.**

19 **JULIA:** *(Smiles.)* **Is there something I could help you find?**

20 **SASHA: She's going to jail over a broken plate?**

21 **JULIA:** *(Points to a sign.)* **You break, you pay. And be sure to**

22   **read the fine print. Now how may I help you?**

23 **SASHA: Forget that. I'm leaving this place before I break**

24   **something.** *(She rushes off, and then we hear a large*

25   *crash. JULIA runs off and pulls SASHA back On-Stage.)*

26   **Look, that was a complete accident. The aisles are so**

27   **narrow and my hand barely touched this little bowl**

28   **and ... I don't know what happened.**

29 **JULIA: That was a Geisha gravy bowl. Do you know what**

30   **that costs?**

31 **SASHA:** *(Holds out her hands.)* **Just go ahead and handcuff**

32   **me because by the look on your face, it's more than**

33   **twenty dollars.**

34 **JULIA: That Geisha gravy bowl is worth three hundred**

35   **and twenty-five dollars. Security!**

1   MACK: *(Enters.)* **The police are on their way to pick up the**
2   **lady who broke the dinner plate. Now what's**
3   **happened?**
4   JULIA: **She broke a Geisha gravy bowl.**
5   MACK: **Not a Geisha.**
6   JULIA: **Yes. A Geisha.**
7   MACK: *(Shakes head.)* **Can you pay?**
8   SASHA: *(Holds out her hands.)* **Take me away.** *(As MACK is*
9   *leading her off)* **Do I get one phone call?**
10 JULIA: *(Looking at the floor)* **What a day. What's wrong**
11   **with these people?** *(Loud crash)* **What now?**
12 MARGIE: *(Enters.)* **Hello. I'm looking for a Petite Rose**
13   **crystal vase.**
14 JULIA: **Did you just break something over there?**
15 MARGIE: **Who, me?**
16 JULIA: **Yes, you. I just heard something fall.**
17 MARGIE: **I didn't hear a thing. So anyway, I'm looking for**
18   **a wedding gift for my niece. She said there was a**
19   **crystal vase on sale that she wanted. I believe it's**
20   **called Petite Rose. Would you happen to have that?**
21 JULIA: **Just a moment while I check.** *(Exits, screams, then*
22   *enters.)* **That was an 1887 Queen Victoria**
23   **commemorative plate that you broke!**
24 MARGIE: *(Looking around)* **Who? Me?**
25 JULIA: **Do you have any idea how much that is worth?**
26 MARGIE: **Who said I did it?**
27 MACK: *(Enters.)* **We have her on the security cameras.**
28   **Picked up the plate, put it down, then set it on the**
29   **corner edge and it came crashing down.**
30 MARGIE: **Me?**
31 JULIA: **That is a rare antique. It cost one thousand, five**
32   **hundred dollars!**
33 MARGIE: *(Nervous laugh)* **Accidents happen. Now, are you**
34   **still going to check on my Petite Rose crystal vase?**
35   **I'm hoping it doesn't cost too much.**

1 JULIA: You break, you pay!
2 MARGIE: But I didn't ...
3 MACK: Ma'am, you did. Security cameras don't lie.
4 MARGIE: I'm not paying for a one thousand, five hundred
5   dollar plate.
6 JULIA: That was a rare 1887 Queen Victoria
7   commemorative plate! You can't just waltz in here
8   and break something and walk out as if it never
9   happened.
10 MARGIE: You can't make me pay for a plate.
11 MACK: Ma'am, our sign clearly states that if you break,
12   you pay.
13 JULIA: And I do accept all major credit cards for your
14   convenience.
15 MARGIE: My only credit card has a thousand dollar limit
16   and that is maxed out. So, I don't see how you are
17   going to make me pay. What kind of store is this,
18   anyways? Can't you just write these accidents off?
19   That's what other stores do.
20 JULIA: Not here we don't. This is a fine china store and we
21   expect our customers to pay for what they purchase
22   or for what they break. I need your payment please.
23   One thousand, five hundred dollars.
24 MARGIE: But I don't have one thousand, five hundred
25   dollars.
26 JULIA: Mack ...
27 MACK: I know the drill. Ma'am, you need to come with me.
28 MARGIE: For what?
29 JULIA: We'll talk about it in my office.
30 MARGIE: But I came here to buy a vase for a wedding gift
31   for my niece. I don't want to go with you.
32 MACK: Don't make me take out my handcuffs.
33 MARGIE: Handcuffs? Are you serious?
34 MACK: Let's go. *(They exit.)*
35 JULIA: These stupid, stupid, clumsy people. They are like

1   **bulls in a china closet. Well, the punishment fits the**

2   **crime. Jail time for those foolish, uncoordinated**

3   **shoppers. And do I care? No!** *(A loud crash is heard.)*

4   **What now!**

5   **MACK:** *(Enters.)* **Miss Julia, I'm taking myself to jail.**

6   **JULIA: Not you, Mack.**

7   **MACK: I don't know what happened. I was escorting Miss**

8   **Margie off to my office and I tripped on my shoelace**

9   **and several plates tipped over, and ... I'm so sorry,**

10   **Miss Julia. I'll miss working for you.**

11 **JULIA: What did you break? What?** *(She rushes Off-Stage.*

12   *From Off-Stage)* **No! Not the Old Willow dinner plates!**

13   **No!** *(A loud crash is heard.)*

14 **MACK: Miss Julia?**

15 **JULIA:** *(Enters.)* **Mack ...**

16 **MACK: Yes, Miss Julia?**

17 **JULIA: Take me with you. I just broke the Ambassador**

18   **Gold Creamer. That would be a month's salary for**

19   **me.**

20 **MACK:** *(Shakes head.)* **Come with me, Miss Julia.**

21 **JULIA: Mack ...**

22 **MACK: Yes, Miss Julia?**

23 **JULIA: Did I ever tell you I hate my job?**

24 **MACK: No, Miss Julia.**

25 **JULIA: Whenever I see the light of freedom, I think I'll go**

26   **to work at McDonalds.**

27 **MACK: Would you like an apple pie with that, ma'am?**

28 **JULIA: Yes. Yes I would.**

7. The Nothing Club

CAST: (3M, 2F) JOHN, AMANDA, SETH, VICTORIA, DYLAN
PROPS: Notebook paper, pen
SETTING: Classroom

1   *(At rise, a student and leader of The Nothing Club is*
2   *speaking to the others.)*
3   **JOHN: Welcome to the first meeting of The Nothing Club.**
4   **I'm John and I've created this club for those of us who**
5   **have no life.**
6   **AMANDA: Thank you. Thank you so much! I feel like I have**
7   **a life now.**
8   **JOHN: Those of us who are in here should not belong to any**
9   **other clubs. Such as the Academic Club, Chemistry**
10   **Club, French Club, Spanish Club, Latin Club, Forensics**
11   **Club, Thespian Club, Chess Club, Computer Club, and**
12   **so on. You should also not be involved in any**
13   **extracurricular activities such as choir, band, theatre,**
14   **dance, sports, and so on. This club was specifically**
15   **designed for us who are involved in nothing. Hence,**
16   **The Nothing Club. So, why don't we go around and**
17   **introduce ourselves?**
18   **AMANDA: I'll go first. I'm Amanda and aside from going to**
19   **school I do nothing. I once tried out for cheerleader in**
20   **the fourth grade, but I didn't make it.** *(Stands.)* **Let me**
21   **show you.** *(Performs a cheer.)* **"Big G, little O. Go! Go! Big**
22   **G, little O. Go! Go! Big G, little O. Go! Go!" Was that**
23   **really all that bad? Anyway, after being overlooked in**
24   **fourth grade, I said forget it. So I guess I'm a wannabe**
25   **cheerleader that has crawled into a hole and refuses to**
26   **be involved in anything. Until now that is.** *(To JOHN)*
27   **Thank you, John, for creating this club for us.**
28   **JOHN: Thank you Amanda for joining us. Who would like to**
29   **go next?**

1 SETH: I guess I will. I'm Seth. And the truth is, I don't
2   really like people. I guess that's why I don't belong to
3   any clubs. It drives my parents crazy. They are always
4   hounding me to get involved in something ...
5   anything! So basically that's why I've joined this club.
6   To get my parents off my back.
7 JOHN: Thank you, Seth. Whatever the reason, we're glad
8   to have you here. Next?
9 VICTORIA: *(Softly)* I guess I'll go next. *(Pause)*
10 JOHN: What's your name?
11 VICTORIA: *(Softly)* Victoria.
12 JOHN: Glad to have you here, Victoria.
13 VICTORIA: *(Softly)* People say I'm shy. I guess I am. And ...
14   well ... I don't really have anything else to say.
15 JOHN: That's all right, Victoria. Next.
16 DYLAN: I'm Dylan and I've tried lots of clubs and
17   activities, but I don't fit in anywhere, you know? So
18   I'm thinking this nothing club might be just the
19   thing for me. 'Cause I like doing nothing. Watching
20   TV, playing video games, napping ... I call it
21   something, but my mom says it's nothing. A waste of
22   time. Actually I like wasting time. So anyway, that's
23   why I'm here. To do nothing in a nothing club.
24 JOHN: Thank you, Dylan. As you see, there are many
25   reasons for being a member of this club. But the one
26   common factor is that all of us have no life. Would
27   you all agree? *(They ALL nod.)*
28 AMANDA: But what will we do in our club?
29 DYLAN: Nothing!
30 VICTORIA: *(Softly)* That's fine with me as long as I don't
31   have to talk.
32 DYLAN: I can bring my headphones and iPod to the
33   meetings and listen to my music.
34 AMANDA: But shouldn't we do *something?*
35 SETH: Well, if we do, let's not venture out too much. Like

1   I said, I don't really like people. And crowds and I
2   don't get along.
3   VICTORIA: *(Softly)* I don't really like people that much,
4   either. They scare me.
5   JOHN: Perhaps we can agree on a few activities. Any
6   suggestions?
7   AMANDA: *(Raises hand.)* I volunteer to be the secretary of
8   our club. I can take notes and keep a calendar of all
9   our upcoming events.
10   JOHN: Thank you, Amanda. That would be helpful.
11   AMANDA: *(Takes out notebook paper and a pen.)* OK, for the
12   rest of this month, what activities should we plan?
13   DYLAN: Nothing is fine with me.
14   SETH: We could make fun of the people who make fun of
15   us.
16   VICTORIA: Is that an activity?
17   SETH: We can make it one.
18   AMANDA: I'll write that down. *(As she is writing)* Make fun
19   of people. We can do that at our next meeting.
20   JOHN: Any other suggestions?
21   DYLAN: Watch TV.
22   SETH: I like TV. Can we do that?
23   JOHN: I'm sure we can. Perhaps we could all bring some
24   snacks, too.
25   AMANDA: I'm putting that down for the seventeenth. TV
26   time and snacks.
27   JOHN: Thank you, Amanda.
28   VICTORIA: *(Softly)* We could go to a restaurant and
29   pretend we are important people showing up for a
30   meeting.
31   DYLAN: If it involves eating, I'm in.
32   SETH: As long as I don't have to talk or socialize too much.
33   Like I said, basically I don't like people.
34   VICTORIA: Maybe you can sit by me, Seth. I don't talk very
35   much.

1   SETH: Perfect. *(They share a smile.)*
2   AMANDA: *(Writing)* Dinner. I'll put that down on the
3   twenty-fourth. Seven p.m. Place TBA.
4   SETH: My parents will be thrilled to see me get out of the
5   house for once.
6   AMANDA: I just thought of something. Maybe we could
7   have a talent show. *(The others moan.)* I could do one
8   of my cheers. *(Stands.)* Like this one! *(Performs a*
9   *cheer.)* "Tigers got the power, Tigers got the heat,
10   Tigers got the spirit, to knock you off your feet!"
11 JOHN: Amanda, the problem with a talent show is that
12   most of us have no talent.
13 VICTORIA: Unless it's a hidden talent.
14 JOHN: Very true, Victoria. Why don't we go around and
15   share our talents, if any.
16 AMANDA: Cheerleading! Even though I wasn't ever
17   picked.
18 SETH: Writing complaint letters. And I do it quite well if
19   you ask me. You know, I've never shared this talent
20   with anyone before. Which means ... I guess I'm
21   bonding with you guys. And anyway, the complaint
22   letters get me lots of coupons for free stuff. Which is
23   an added bonus. "Your product stinks! It did not
24   meet my expectations and I want my money back! I
25   look forward to your reply and a resolution to my
26   problem and will allow one week before contacting
27   the Better Business Bureau. Thank you. Sincerely,
28   Seth Carmichael."
29 VICTORIA: *(Softly)* I guess I have a hidden talent.
30 JOHN: Tell us about it, Victoria.
31 VICTORIA: Well, I like to cut split ends off my hair. *(Holds*
32   *out a portion of her hair.)* See how shiny and pretty it
33   is?
34 DYLAN: Isn't that more of a hobby?
35 VICTORIA: I think it's a talent. *(To JOHN)* Can't cutting

1   split ends be a talent?

2 JOHN: Yes, I think so.

3 DYLAN: OK, well my talent is quitting. I quit this. I quit
4   that. I've started so many projects, goals,
5   memberships, you name it, it's unreal! I quit before I
6   have the chance to succeed. So I say if cutting split
7   ends is a talent then being a quitter is one too.

8 AMANDA: What about you, John? What is your talent?

9 JOHN: Procrastination. I can do anything and everything
10   imaginable before getting down to the task at hand.
11   Now granted, procrastination might not be a talent,
12   but if it could be, then I have mastered it.

13 AMANDA: But you're the president of The Nothing Club.
14   How can this be?

15 JOHN: True. But knowing how I am, I'll manage to find
16   something else to do besides planning the topics for
17   our next meeting. Believe me, I'll find something
18   better to do. So it will be a nothing club. Nothing
19   planned. Nothing to talk about. And nothing to share.

20 DYLAN: Works for me.

21 SETH: Me too.

22 VICTORIA: As long as I don't have to talk, I'm OK.

23 JOHN: And speaking of our next meeting, I may not be
24   able to make it.

25 DYLAN: Me too. Seeing how I'm a quitter and I don't stick
26   with anything.

27 SETH: I can't be at the next meeting either. Like I said, I
28   typically don't like people. Don't take it personally,
29   but to be honest, I don't think I like any of you.

30 VICTORIA: If none of you are coming, then I'm not either.
31   Because that means it'd just be me and Amanda. Just
32   the two of us. Then she'd expect me to talk to her. And
33   I don't like to talk. So no, I can't make the next
34   meeting either.

35 AMANDA: Well, it sounds like I'll be here by myself next

1 week. I guess I'll just have to work on my
2 **cheerleading routines then.** *(Stands to cheer.)* **"Our**
3 **team is red hot. Our team is red hot. Our team is R-E-**
4 **D, H-O-T hot. Once we start we can't be stopped!"** *(She*
5 *finishes with an awkward jump. The others clap.)*
6 **JOHN: Well, this concludes our first meeting. See you next**
7 **week. That is, if I can make it.**
8 **SETH: Great. I'm out of here. And probably won't be back.**
9 *(Exits.)*
10 **DYLAN: Later, guys.** *(Exits.)*
11 **VICTORIA:** *(Softy)* **Bye. I'm leaving now.**
12 **AMANDA:** *(Shrugs and decides to do her cheer again.)* **"Our**
13 **team is red hot. Our team is red hot. Our team is R-E-**
14 **D, H-O-T hot. Once we start we can't be stopped!"** *(She*
15 *finishes with an awkward jump.)* **I think I'm a great**
16 **cheerleader.**

8. Grounded Until Further Notice

CAST: (1M, 1F) DANNY, HANNAH
PROPS: Schoolbooks, notebook paper
SETTING: Danny's bedroom

1　*(At rise, DANNY is alone in his bedroom. His schoolbooks*
2　*and notebook paper surround him.)*
3　**DANNY:** It's like the world has stopped. It's so quiet. So very,
4　　very quiet. The chatting, gone. The constant feeding of
5　　activities, updates, thoughts, photos ... gone. The links,
6　　the friend requests ... all gone. I wonder what everyone
7　　is doing? This is not fair! No phone. No computer. No
8　　TV. No life! I'm all alone. Alone knowing the pathetic
9　　and depressing status lingering beside my name. My
10　　status? *Grounded until further notice!*
11　**HANNAH:** *(Enters.)* Are you talking to yourself?
12　**DANNY:** Hannah! Little sister. Come in. Come in!
13　**HANNAH:** Wow. You usually don't invite me into your room.
14　**DANNY:** *(Pulling her into his room)* Come sit down. Talk to
15　　me!
16　**HANNAH:** Mom doesn't ground you for not cleaning your
17　　room?
18　**DANNY:** I am grounded.
19　**HANNAH:** I know. Until further notice. I saw that on
20　　Facebook.
21　**DANNY:** But I'm not grounded for my dirty room.
22　**HANNAH:** You should be. Then what are you grounded for?
23　**DANNY:** American history. Current grade: twenty-three.
24　**HANNAH:** Man! That's terrible. A twenty-three? No wonder
25　　you're grounded.
26　**DANNY:** But Hannah, it's not my fault.
27　**HANNAH:** I bet you tried that one out on Mom. And I bet it
28　　didn't work.
29　**DANNY:** It's my teacher's fault. Mr. Adams is always giving

1   out these pop quizzes. And totally without any
2   warning.
3 HANNAH: That's what pop quizzes are about, big brother.
4 DANNY: Well, I'm not good at tests. Especially ones I
5   haven't studied for.
6 HANNAH: *(Patting his back)* That's why you're supposed to
7   pay attention during class. So you'll be prepared.
8 DANNY: I know, *Mom!* But it's like Mr. Adams will give you
9   one question and if you blow it ... well hello zero! Like
10   yesterday, the question was, "The Statue of Liberty is
11   a gift from which country?"
12 HANNAH: France.
13 DANNY: You know that?
14 HANNAH: Of course. And you don't know that?
15 DANNY: Well, I know it *now.*
16 HANNAH: What'd you say?
17 DANNY: Canada.
18 HANNAH: *(Laughs.)* Dummy. Try another one on me.
19 DANNY: OK, Miss Smarty Pants. What is the day that will
20   live in infamy?
21 HANNAH: The attack on Pearl Harbor.
22 DANNY: Show off.
23 HANNAH: Your answer was?
24 DANNY: When Elvis died.
25 HANNAH: Stupid! Give me another one.
26 DANNY: What year did the Boston Tea Party take place?
27 HANNAH: Easy. 1773.
28 DANNY: Right again.
29 HANNAH: And your answer?
30 DANNY: 1973.
31 HANNAH: You are so dumb!
32 DANNY: Thanks, sis. Enough of American history.
33 HANNAH: Aren't you supposed to be studying?
34 DANNY: I have been.
35 HANNAH: Uh-huh. Sure.

1 DANNY: What else is there to do? I can't get on the
2   computer. Mom took my phone away. No TV.
3 HANNAH: That would totally freak me out. I couldn't live
4   like that.
5 DANNY: Hannah, I'm going crazy in here.
6 HANNAH: I bet. And it stinks in here, too.
7 DANNY: I miss my social network life. I'm dying to know
8   what everyone's status is right now. "Hanging with
9   Tim at the arcade." "Just woke up ... dreamed I was
10   Pokémon." "Woooo! I just got my car windows tinted
11   and now I look super bad." "I just ate some alligator
12   meat and it was awesome." "Doing the funky monkey
13   dance." "Ugh ... I hate studying." I can relate to that!
14   Me? "Grounded until further notice."
15 HANNAH: *(Picks up history book.)* You should be studying.
16   I'll leave you alone so you can.
17 DANNY: No, Hannah. Don't leave me!
18 HANNAH: Since when do you want to hang out with me?
19 DANNY: Hannah, I'm lonely. I'm not used to going without
20   my phone and computer. I feel like I'm in solitary
21   confinement and the walls are closing in on me.
22 HANNAH: Well, Danny, you did this to yourself. A twenty-
23   three in American history is pretty bad.
24 DANNY: I know. I know. But I hate history. I want to live in
25   the present. The here and now. Forget the past.
26 HANHAH: Well, if you don't want to be a prisoner in your
27   room and go without chatting up your people, then
28   you better crack open this book and study.
29 DANNY: Hannah, I'm taking a break.
30 HANNAH: Uh-huh.
31 DANNY: And I'm dying to know what's going on with
32   everyone. I feel like the whole world is passing me by.
33 HANNAH: I have an idea. *(Opens book.)* Time for a pop
34   quiz.
35 DANNY: You're going to quiz me?

1　HANNAH: I'm helping you get started. Forget Facebook
2　　　and think American history. Question: What begins
3　　　with, "We the people..."?
4　DANNY: Uh ...uh ... Oh, I forgot.
5　HANNAH: The U.S. Constitution. Now remember that!
6　DANNY: OK, I'll try
7　HANNAH: Question: Who said, "Give me liberty or give
8　　　me death"?
9　DANNY: Uh ...uh ... Patrick ...
10　HANNAH: Come on. You're close.
11　DANNY: Patrick Swayze?
12　HANNAH: Patrick Henry. Oh my gosh. You are so stupid!
13　DANNY: *(Grabs book.)* I know. I need to study.
14　HANNAH: And clean your room because it really stinks in
15　　　here. I'm leaving.
16　DANNY: Wait! Wait!
17　HANNAH: What?
18　DANNY: *(Holds out book.)* One more. Give me one more
19　　　question.
20　HANNAH: *(Reluctantly opens book.)* What war was fought
21　　　in the U.S. between the North and the South?
22　DANNY: Oh, boy. That's a hard one.
23　HANNAH: No it's not. It's easy. *(Trying to help)* The ... Civ ...
24　　　Civ.
25　DANNY: The Civil War!
26　HANNAH: Correct.
27　DANNY: Yes!
28　HANNAH: *(Turns page.)* Who gave the Gettysburg Address
29　　　speech?
30　DANNY: Uh ...Uh ...
31　HANNAH: *(Trying to help)* Abe ... Abe ...
32　DANNY: Abraham Lincoln!
33　HANNAH: Correct. *(Turns page.)* What ship carried the
34　　　Pilgrims to America in 1620?
35　DANNY: Uh ...Uh ... Let me think. Was it the Pinta?

1   HANNAH: *(Shakes head.)* **May ... May ...**

2   **DANNY: The Mayflower!**

3   **HANNAH: Correct.**

4   **DANNY: Yes!**

5   **HANNAH: Now see if you can get this one all by yourself.**

6   **DANNY: OK. I'm ready.**

7   **HANNAH: The Fourth of July was the day that what**

8   **happened?**

9   **DANNY: Uh ... Uh ...**

10   **HANNAH: Come on! You can do this. We celebrate it every**

11   **year. Red, white, and blue. Fireworks ...**

12   **DANNY: Hot dogs and homemade ice cream.**

13   **HANNAH: Forget the hot dogs and homemade ice cream.**

14   **What happened on the Fourth of July?**

15   **DANNY: Uh ... Uh ...** *(Suddenly)* **The Declaration of**

16   **Independence!**

17   **HANNAH:** *(Slams book shut.)* **Correct!**

18   **DANNY: Yes! I got it.**

19   **HANNAH: I'm leaving now. Your room smells too nasty for**

20   **me to stay in here any longer.** *(She exits.)*

21   **DANNY:** *(To himself)* **I'm not so dumb after all. Fourth of**

22   **July ... the Declaration of Independence.** *(Opens*

23   *book.)* **I'll test myself one more time. "Who**

24   **assassinated Abraham Lincoln?** *(Closes book, but*

25   *holds his place.)* **That would be John Wilkes Booth.**

26   *(Opens book.)* **Yes! Yes, yes, yes! New status update: I**

27   **have conquered American history!** *(As he exits)* **Hey,**

28   **Mom! Mom! You can un-ground me now!**

9. Barney

CAST: (2F) JADE, NORA
SETTING: Jade's bedroom

1   JADE: Nora, I'm so glad you came over. I've got to tell you
2   something. It's a secret.
3   NORA: Oh, I love secrets. Tell me! Tell me!
4   JADE: I got a tattoo.
5   NORA: What? How? When?
6   JADE: This weekend.
7   NORA: You're lying.
8   JADE: No! But I did lie about my age. I said I was eighteen.
9   And lucky me, they didn't ask for identification.
10 NORA: No! Are you serious?
11 JADE: Do I look eighteen?
12 NORA: No. I don't know. Maybe. Really? You got a tattoo? Oh
13   my gosh! You're so lucky. Everyone will be so jealous.
14 JADE: I know! But yes, I did it. I have a tattoo. But there's
15   only one little problem.
16 NORA: What's that?
17 JADE: My mom. If she ever finds out ... she'll kill me.
18 NORA: Just hide it from her. I hide things from my mom all
19   the time. So tell me, where is it?
20 JADE: My ankle.
21 NORA: Awesome! But I guess you'll have to wear pants
22   around your mom all the time, huh?
23 JADE: I know. But there is one problem about that.
24 NORA: What?
25 JADE: Next weekend we're going to my Aunt Karen's
26   wedding. Her fourth actually. And believe it or not, it's
27   this humongous church wedding. She spent thousands
28   of dollars on a wedding that everyone says won't last.
29   But that's not the point. I'm one of the six bridesmaids
30   who has to wear a tea-length dress.

1 NORA: Uh-oh. That's not good. Then everyone will see
2   what's on your ankle.
3 JADE: I know! Now I wish I'd waited until after the
4   wedding to lie about my age and get a tattoo.
5 NORA: That would have been better timing.
6 JADE: And it's not like it won't show. I mean, it is colorful.
7 NORA: Oh, let me see it.
8 JADE: *(Raises her pant leg to show NORA. Smiles.)* Do you
9   like it?
10 NORA: What is that?
11 JADE: What do you mean, "What is it?" It's a dinosaur.
12 NORA: A purple and green dinosaur?
13 JADE: Yes! Don't you like it?
14 NORA: Barney? You put Barney on your ankle?
15 JADE: No! That's not Barney. It's just a dinosaur. A purple
16   and green dinosaur.
17 NORA: It looks like Barney.
18 JADE: No it doesn't.
19 NORA: Yes it does. And do you know what it reminds me
20   of?
21 JADE: No. What?
22 NORA: That song. *(Sings.)* "I love you ... you love me ... we're
23   a happy family ... "
24 JADE: Nora! Stop it!
25 NORA: Jade, why did you put Barney on your ankle when
26   you could've gotten a butterfly or a cross or a
27   friendship heart? But Barney? Really? Barney is
28   stupid!
29 JADE: Nora, it's not Barney.
30 NORA: Let me see it again. Maybe I looked at it wrong.
31 JADE: *(JADE lifts her pant leg.)* See.
32 NORA: Yeah, I see.
33 JADE: And?
34 NORA: I'm sorry, but that looks like Barney to me.
35 JADE: No it doesn't! It's just a colorful dinosaur. I picked it

1   out. The tattoo artist never said anything about it
2   looking like Barney. He said *(Deep voice)* "Yeah, I can
3   see that on you. Cool." The tattoo artist thought it was
4   cool.

5 NORA: And ... on a positive note ... whenever you have
6   kids, they will love it. That is, if Barney is still
7   popular. Is he still popular? I remember watching
8   him with my little brother. I don't even know if he's
9   still on TV. He might be old news. And honestly, I
10   never liked Barney. I thought he was kind of weird
11   and creepy looking.

12 JADE: Nora, I'm telling you for the last time ... It's not
13   Barney!

14 NORA: OK. OK. But I'm just wondering ...

15 JADE: What?

16 NORA: I'm just wondering if you'll still like having a
17   dinosaur on your ankle when you're old. Like thirty
18   or forty years old.

19 JADE: I don't know. How would I know that?

20 NORA: Or when you're really old like fifty or sixty and
21   you're walking around in your grandma nightgown
22   and you look down and there he is. Barney!

23 JADE: It's not Barney.

24 NORA: The purple and green dinosaur. Do you think it
25   will blend in with your pink and white cotton gown?
26   And he might start to sag. Which I heard that
27   happens. Because you know, old people's skin sags.
28   And you might even have some stubbly ole black
29   hairs growing out of Barney's body. But you know, if
30   you like him, well, good for you.

31 JADE: For the millionth time ... I did not get Barney the
32   dinosaur on my ankle.

33 NORA: OK, OK! It's just a purple and green dinosaur that
34   looks like Barney. *(Sings.)* "I love you ... you love me ...
35   we're a happy family!" Do you like that song?

1   JADE: No!
2   NORA: You know, I don't either. And I think if I got a tattoo
3   I'd get a dragonfly. I heard they are associated with
4   good luck and are considered the power of light. That
5   would be pretty magical. Don't you think? But a
6   purple and green dinosaur? No, I wouldn't want
7   something cartoon-ish like that.
8   JADE: My dinosaur is not cartoon-ish.
9   NORA: Well, kinda. Because I don't think real life
10   dinosaurs were purple and green.
11 JADE: How do you know? You weren't alive back then! And
12   did you see Cory's tattoo? He got a Superman tattoo.
13 NORA: That was airbrushed.
14 JADE: No it wasn't. I saw it. It looked real.
15 NORA: No, it was airbrushed. He did it at the fair last
16   month. It's already faded and gone. You didn't know
17   that?
18 JADE: No! Cory was telling everyone his Superman tattoo
19   was real.
20 NORA: Cory lied.
21 JADE: I lied. Said I was eighteen. Now I have a dinosaur
22   tattoo on my ankle.
23 NORA: And it will be there forever and ever and ever.
24 JADE: Oh, Nora! My mom is going to kill me.
25 NORA: I bet. My mom would totally flip out. She might
26   even disown me.
27 JADE: Oh, what am I going to do?
28 NORA: I know! Cover it with a Band-Aid. Tell her you cut
29   yourself shaving.
30 JADE: She won't allow me to wear a big Band-Aid on my
31   ankle during Aunt Karen's wedding. She spent a lot of
32   money on my bridesmaid dress.
33 NORA: What color is it the dress?
34 JADE: Why?
35 NORA: Just wondering.

1 JADE: Light blue.

2 NORA: Light blue with a purple and green dinosaur? No,
3   that's going to clash.

4 JADE: Oh, what did I do?

5 NORA: Too bad you can't scrub it off.

6 JADE: I could try.

7 NORA: It wouldn't work. But we can look at the bright
8   side.

9 JADE: What bright side?

10 NORA: Well, if you love Barney ... I mean, the dinosaur,
11   then it doesn't matter what anyone else thinks.

12 JADE: Think that logic will work with my mom?

13 NORA: No. Probably not. Because if she's anything like my
14   mom, she will scream, cry, and then scream some
15   more. And it could go on for days or weeks or even
16   months. But then, your life will eventually return to
17   normal. And when it does, you need to remember
18   that you love Barney ... I mean you love your purple
19   and green dinosaur.

20 JADE: Why?

21 NORA: Because it will speak confidence. Like you meant
22   to put Barney on your ankle. And you're proud to
23   have him there. And this summer when you are
24   wearing your bathing suit to the swimming pool,
25   never mind the people who are staring at your ankle.
26   Just walk around as if you are proud to have Barney,
27   I mean, the dinosaur on your ankle.

28 JADE: Oh, why didn't I think this through? What have I
29   done?

30 NORA: And when those little kids at the swimming pool
31   see Barney on your ankle ... they will all chase you
32   around the pool. "Barney! Barney! I see Barney!
33   Mommy, look! It's Barney!"

34 JADE: It's not Barney!

35 NORA: "Mommy, I want to touch Barney!" And then they

1   will probably start singing. "I love you ... you love me

2   ... we're a happy family ... "

3 JADE: *(Covers her ears.)* What have I done?

4 NORA: You know, I really hate that song, but now it's stuck

5   in my head. "I love you ... you love me ... we're a happy

6   family!"

7 JADE: Stop it! Stop it! Please, stop it!

8 NORA: I'm sorry, but I can't. I can't get that song out of my

9   head. "I love you, you love me, we're a happy

10   family ... "

11 JADE: My tattoo is not Barney. I hate Barney. Everyone

12   hates Barney! Oh, what have I done.

13 NORA: "I love you, you love me, we're a happy family ... "

10. Stranded

CAST: (2M, 2F) PHIL, CLAY, ANNA, CHLOE
PROPS: Purses for Anna and Chloe, package of two saltine
  crackers, peppermint candy, Tic Tac mints
SETTING: Phil's car

1   *(At rise, PHIL and CLAY are sitting in the front seat of*
2   *PHIL's car. PHIL is in the driver's seat and CLAY is in the*
3   *passenger's seat. ANNA and CHLOE are sitting in the*
4   *backseat. They often lean forward when they speak to the*
5   *boys.)*
6   **PHIL: I think I drove a good fifteen miles on just the fumes.**
7   **CLAY: At least.**
8   **PHIL: And now, out of gas.**
9   **CLAY: I love being stranded.**
10 **PHIL: You do?**
11 **CLAY: No!**
12 **ANNA:** *(Leans forward.)* **Where are we?**
13 **PHIL: I'm not sure.**
14 **CLAY: Looks like the middle of nowhere.**
15 **CHLOE:** *(Leans forward.)* **We're stuck in the middle of**
16   **nowhere?**
17 **PHIL: Relax. I called my dad. He's bringing a gas can.**
18 **CLAY: But do you think he understands where we are?**
19   **Because you don't seem to know where we are.**
20 **PHIL: I told Dad that we were headed south on Farm Market**
21   **Road Eighty-Two, towards the river. Then somewhere**
22   **along the way, I took a right, then a couple of winding**
23   **roads, which I shouldn't have done ... seeing that I got a**
24   **little turned around ... and then we ended up here. On**
25   **this dirt road with no street signs, road signs, or any**
26   **signs to point us in the right direction. But if anyone**
27   **can find us, my dad can find us.**
28 **ANNA:** *(Leans forward.)* **Next time, remind me to remind you**

1   to check your fuel gauge before we head out on our
2   next adventure.

3 CHLOE: *(Leans forward.)* And remind me to bring a
4   survival kit. Like soft drinks and candy. Because I'm
5   hungry.

6 ANNA: Me too.

7 PHIL: Relax. My dad will be here soon.

8 CLAY: Maybe.

9 CHLOE: Maybe we should make an SOS sign out of sticks.

10 ANNA: And build a big fire so he can see us.

11 PHIL: My dad will find us. He said he'd call when he felt
12   like he was close. Then I'll look around and tell him
13   what I see so he can know where to go.

14 CLAY: *(Looking around)* Let's see. There are lots of rocks. A
15   few trees. And no sign of the river.

16 ANNA: We're going to be stuck here forever, aren't we?

17 PHIL: No!

18 CHLOE: Does anyone in here have anything to eat?

19 ANNA: I have a saltine cracker in my purse.

20 CHLOE: One?

21 ANNA: I think there are two in the package. It came with
22   my salad and I didn't eat them, so I threw it in my
23   purse for a rainy day.

24 CHLOE: Good. Because we may have to survive on those
25   crackers for a few days.

26 ANNA: A few days?

27 CHLOE: You never know. I've heard of people getting lost
28   for a few days or even weeks before being found. We
29   have to prepare for the worst. So I say tomorrow we
30   divide one saltine cracker between the four of us. It
31   won't be much, but it's better than nothing.

32 CLAY: And what are we supposed to do when we get
33   thirsty, Chloe?

34 CHLOE: We'll, I guess we will have to survive by drinking
35   the dew off the leaves.

1 PHIL: I'm not licking dew off leaves.
2 ANNA: You're making me thirsty right now.
3 CHLOE: Does anyone have anything else to eat? We need
4   to gather our food supplies and see what we have.
5 ANNA: Let me check my purse and see if I have anything
6   else. Here are the two saltine crackers. *(Hands the*
7   *package to CHLOE.)* Oh! I have a piece of peppermint
8   candy.
9 CHLOE: *(Takes the candy.)* Thank you. If needed, we can
10   crush it with a rock and suck on the small pieces for
11   energy.
12 PHIL: And fresh breath! *(The BOYS laugh.)*
13 CHLOE: Anyone else have any food for survival?
14 CLAY: Uh ... there's a couple of ketchup packages in
15   between the seats here.
16 CHLOE: Hand them to me.
17 PHIL: Yeah! We can each suck half a package of ketchup
18   for one meal. That should be plenty of nourishment
19   to keep up going.
20 CLAY: Then slurp dew off the leaves. Hey, we're gonna live
21   after all.
22 CHLOE: Maybe not. We only have two crackers. That will
23   only last for a couple of days. We may have to think
24   about eating bark from the trees.
25 PHIL: Can you do that? Eat bark from trees for survival?
26 CHLOE: I don't know. I think so.
27 ANNA: How long do you think we're going to be stranded?
28 CHLOE: Anna, it could be days. Or even weeks.
29 ANNA: But I have a chemistry test on Friday that I can't
30   miss. No retakes! And I need the grade.
31 CHLOE: I understand. But the most important thing to
32   concentrate on right now is survival. Living. *(Looking*
33   *out the window)* Not becoming a wild animal's next
34   meal. And learning how to survive with the few
35   resources we have.

1 CLAY: Two saltine crackers, ketchup, and a piece of
2   peppermint candy.
3 PHIL: And slurping dew drops off leaves.
4 CHLOE: Because ultimately, being alive is more important
5   than a chemistry test, Anna. Wouldn't you agree?
6 ANNA: Yeah, but I might end up failing chemistry if I can't
7   be there for the test. A zero is going to bring my grade
8   to below passing.
9 CHLOE: But your life is so much more important.
10 ANNA: I know.
11 CLAY: Hey! You know what? We'll probably be on TV. I bet
12   all of the major news stations will cover the story of
13   four teens who are lost in the woods.
14 PHIL: This isn't exactly the woods.
15 CLAY: Well, they always sensationalize everything. And by
16   the time we are rescued, we'll become heroes. The
17   media will surround us. Microphones shoved in our
18   faces. Camera crews on the scene. "Teens found
19   unharmed, but in dire health as they survived on
20   only two saltine crackers, ketchup, and one piece of
21   peppermint candy for fourteen days."
22 ANNA: I don't want to be stuck in this car for fourteen
23   days.
24 CLAY: But think of the attention we'll get. It'll be on
25   national news.
26 PHIL: I hope they leave out the part about why we are
27   stranded.
28 CLAY: Hiking in the Amazon.
29 CHLOE: That's dumb. The Amazon isn't even in this
30   country.
31 CLAY: Hikers stranded on County Road ... What's the name
32   of this road?
33 PHIL: I don't know. It's a dirt road. I don't think it has a
34   name.
35 CLAY: Hikers stranded ...

1 ANNA: Don't you mean car stranded after running out of
2   gas?
3 CLAY: *(Ignoring her)* Forced to brave the freezing night
4   temperatures ...
5 ANNA: It doesn't drop below fifty or sixty here.
6 CLAY: Eating plants and tree bark for food.
7 CHLOE: That's a high possibility with our low food supply.
8   *(Looking in her purse)* Oh, look! I found some Tic
9   Tacs. I can add this to our survival food bank.
10 PHIL: Tic Tacs?
11 CLAY: Less than two calories per mint. We're going to be
12   skinny and have fresh breath.
13 ANNA: That's stupid.
14 CLAY: And be famous. *(As if holding a microphone up to*
15   *PHIL's mouth)* Tell us about your experience.
16 PHIL: *(Hand to forehead)* It was dreadful! The freezing
17   nights were so brutal. And at night, wild animals
18   surrounded us, hoping we'd become their next meal.
19   And the hunger was hard to bear. But we survived by
20   eating plants and bark and drinking the morning
21   dew from the leaves.
22 CHLOE: And how did you find yourself in this situation?
23 ANNA: By the irresponsible act of my friend not checking
24   his gas gauge.
25 CHLOE: You ran out of gas?
26 ANNA: Exactly.
27 CHLOE: I'm sorry, but this story is not worthy for our
28   viewers. Running a vehicle on an empty gas tank and
29   becoming stranded on a dirt road is not the kind of
30   story we're looking for.
31 CLAY: *(Turns around.)* Oh, you'll see. The media will be all
32   over this!
33 ANNA: Maybe if we turn up missing for a long time.
34 CHLOE: And truthfully ... we could.
35 ANNA: Can you imagine how smelly we would be after a

1   few days of sitting in this car?

2   CHLOE: Ooooh!

3   PHIL: But we'll have fresh breath. Can I have a Tic Tac?

4   CHLOE: No! We have to ration our food.

5   PHIL: Tic Tacs aren't food.

6   ANNA: They are in class when you're really hungry and
7   that's all you have.

8   CHLOE: It's what's for dinner. One Tic Tac apiece.

9   CLAY: Well, I might just pass and go catch me a possum or
10   something to eat.

11   CHLOE: With what?

12   CLAY: *(Cracks knuckles.)* My bare hands.

13   ANNA: I'm hungry. But I don't want to eat any possum.

14   CHLOE: I'd rather have a hamburger.

15   CLAY: Well, seeing how McDonalds is nowhere to be found
16   ... you ladies may have to survive on a little possum
17   stew.

18   ANNA: Yuck! No!

19   CHLOE: Maybe we could have our cracker ration now
20   since everyone is so hungry. *(She breaks the cracker*
21   *into four pieces and hands them out. They quietly*
22   *munch on their little piece of cracker.)*

23   PHIL: Hey, there's my dad!

24   CLAY: *(Throws cracker out the window.)* Great! And when
25   we get back to town, I'm going to buy the biggest,
26   juiciest hamburger I can find!

27   PHIL: Great idea!

28   ANNA: *(Throws cracker out window.)* I want one too!

29   CHLOE: *(Throws cracker out window.)* Me, too! *(Shakes the*
30   *box of Tic Tacs.)* Anyone want a Tic Tac?

11. Confessions

CAST: (2M, 5F) MOLLY, PIPER, VIOLET, ETHAN, RILEY,
  JOEY, CLAIRE
PROPS: A sign that reads "Confessions $1.00," dollar bills
SETTING: Lunchroom

1   *(At rise, MOLLY and PIPER sit at a table in the lunchroom.*
2   *The sign is taped to the front of their table.)*
3   **MOLLY: This isn't working.**
4   **PIPER: Trust me, Molly, it will. We've only been sitting in**
5   **the cafeteria for five minutes.**
6   **MOLLY: But everyone is eating. They aren't interested in**
7   **confessing their sins.**
8   **PIPER: Give it a chance. It has to work because we need**
9   **money to buy those concert tickets.**
10 **MOLLY: I know, Piper, but your other ideas have not panned**
11   **out so well. Selling homemade cookies was a disaster.**
12   **The Red Cross was giving them out free in their "Give**
13   **Blood" campaign the same day we were selling our**
14   **store-bought snickerdoodles. And selling bookmarks in**
15   **the library made people laugh at us. Then selling**
16   **answers to math problems in Mrs. Tyler's room got us**
17   **sent to the principal's office. Now this?**
18 **PIPER: Molly, give it some time. We can't give up after five**
19   **minutes of trying.**
20 **MOLLY: Piper, most people go to church to confess their**
21   **sins. And it's for free.**
22 **PIPER: Well, I believe that lunchtime is the perfect time for**
23   **teenagers to clear their conscience. And you know as**
24   **well as I do that teenagers have a lot to confess.**
25 **MOLLY: True, but personally I wouldn't want to tell anyone**
26   **else about how I messed up. In fact, I wouldn't want**
27   **anyone to know.**
28 **PIPER: But don't you want to clear your conscience?**

1 **MOLLY:** **That's what my diary is for.**

2 **VIOLET:** *(Approaches the table and holds out a dollar.)* **I**
3   **need to confess.**

4 **PIPER:** *(To MOLLY)* **I told you this would work.** *(Takes the*
5   *dollar.)* **Thank you. You may now confess your sins.**

6 **VIOLET: Can I just blurt it out?**

7 **MOLLY: Of course.**

8 **VIOLET:** *(Quickly)* **I cheated on my biology test.** *(Deep*
9   *breath)* **Whew. I said it.**

10 **PIPER: Thank you very much and please come again.**

11 **VIOLET: That's it?**

12 **PIPER: Do you have another confession? That will be**
13   **another dollar please.**

14 **VIOLET: Don't you want to hear the details?**

15 **MOLLY: Sure! I'd like hear how you cheated on your**
16   **biology test.**

17 **VIOLET: OK, so I wrote the answers down in itty-bitty**
18   **print on a piece of note card, wrapped it in a tissue,**
19   **then slipped it in my shirt pocket. Then when the test**
20   **started, I sneezed, pulled out my tissue ... and of**
21   **course my note card, and ... Well, you know the rest.**
22   **And now I feel so guilty.**

23 **MOLLY: Did you pass the test?**

24 **VIOLET: Aced it.**

25 **PIPER: And had you not cheated?**

26 **VIOLET: Let me just say that I do not retain information**
27   **well. I needed a cheat sheet.**

28 **MOLLY: But that's not right. How can you sleep at night?**

29 **VIOLET: I can't. That's why I'm here.**

30 **PIPER: So you cheated ...**

31 **VIOLET: Yes.**

32 **PIPER: And you confessed ...**

33 **VIOLET: Yes.**

34 **PIPER: Well, end of story! Thank you and come again.**

35 **VIOLET: Really? That's it?**

1 PIPER: I'm sorry, but we don't offer advice.

2 MOLLY: But my advice to you ... don't do it again.

3 PIPER: Molly, we don't offer advice.

4 MOLLY: I know, but she needed to hear that.

5 PIPER: *(To VIOLET)* Again, let me thank you for your
6   confession and remind you that confessing is healing
7   to the soul.

8 MOLLY: That sounded good.

9 PIPER: Thank you. *(VIOLET exits. ETHAN enters.)*

10 ETHAN: I need to make a confession.

11 MOLLY: One dollar, please.

12 ETHAN: *(Hands MOLLY a dollar bill.)* Here you go.

13 MOLLY: Thank you.

14 PIPER: You may now confess your sins.

15 ETHAN: OK, here it is. I lied to my mother.

16 PIPER: You're forgiven.

17 ETHAN: Already?

18 MOLLY: *(To ETHAN)* I've done that, too. Actually yesterday.

19 PIPER: *(To MOLLY)* Maybe you need to pay me a dollar.

20 MOLLY: Nah. I don't feel guilty about it.

21 PIPER: You should.

22 MOLLY: It was justified.

23 PIPER: How's that?

24 MOLLY: Well, my mother asked me how I liked the new
25   shower curtain she'd just hung in the bathroom and
26   I said I loved it, but that was a lie. See, it was this
27   clear curtain with black, red, and yellow circles all
28   over it. Talk about ugly.

29 PIPER: Doesn't sound like my taste either.

30 MOLLY: And I said, "Mom, I love it! It's awesome!"

31 ETHAN: Why did you say that?

32 MOLLY: Because I could tell she was all excited about her
33   black, red, and yellow masterpiece of a shower
34   curtain and I wasn't going to burst her bubble.
35   Besides, I needed her to be happy when I asked her if

1   I could borrow twenty dollars. Which she gave to me,
2   by the way.

3   **PIPER:** Good thinking.

4   **MOLLY:** I know.

5   **ETHAN:** Excuse me, can I have my dollar's worth here?

6   **PIPER:** As I recall, you confessed that you lied to your
7   mother. And I replied that you had been forgiven.

8   **MOLLY:** I forgive you, too.

9   **ETHAN:** The forgiveness of you two doesn't change what I
10   did.

11 **PIPER:** Perhaps not, but the important factor here is that
12   you confessed. You cleared your conscience.

13 **MOLLY:** Which is healing to the soul.

14 **ETHAN:** Maybe, but I need to explain why I lied to my
15   mom.

16 **MOLLY:** *(To PIPER)* We should have planned on charging
17   extra for explanations. This could get time
18   consuming.

19 **ETHAN:** So anyway, my mother asked if I knew what
20   happened to the couch. There was this big black stain
21   on it. And I said no. But that was a lie. I'm the one that
22   caused the stain on the couch. My fault! I sat in grease
23   outside, then not thinking, sat on the couch. I did it!
24   And do you know who I blamed it on?

25 **PIPER:** Who?

26 **ETHAN:** My little brother. I said, "Mom, that looks like
27   something Mikey would do."

28 **MOLLY:** You blamed your little brother for something you
29   did?

30 **ETHAN:** Yes! And Mom was freaking out because she
31   couldn't get the stain off her beautiful fancy white
32   couch. She was wiping, crying, cussing. Oh, and my
33   poor brother. When Mikey came inside from playing,
34   it was not a pretty sight. *(Shakes head.)* She tore into
35   him like a hungry lion attacking a wildebeest.

1 PIPER: You're forgiven. Thank you and come again.

2 ETHAN: But wait! Wait. I need to know, should I tell my
3   mom the truth?

4 PIPER: I'm sorry, but we don't offer advice.

5 ETHAN: Well, that's not fair.

6 PIPER: Maybe for another dollar.

7 ETHAN: Forget it. Some confession people you are. *(Exits.)*

8 PIPER: Well, he had a bad attitude.

9 MOLLY: I know. And I feel sorry for his little brother for
10   getting into trouble for something he did. I think we
11   should have told him to tell his mother the truth.

12 PIPER: Molly, we do not offer advice. We are just the ears
13   of the sinners.

14 RILEY: *(Enters. Hands MOLLY a dollar.)* I have a confession.

15 MOLLY: *(Takes dollar.)* Thank you.

16 PIPER: You may now confess your sins.

17 RILEY: I kissed Joey Leatherwood.

18 MOLLY: You did? Oh, he's so cute!

19 PIPER: But Joey Leatherwood has a girlfriend.

20 RILEY: I know. And I have a boyfriend.

21 MOLLY: Uh-oh.

22 PIPER: You're forgiven. Thank you and please come
23   again.

24 MOLLY: I bet Joey is a good kisser, isn't he?

25 RILEY: Oh, he is.

26 MOLLY: Are you going to kiss him again?

27 RILEY: I hope so.

28 PIPER: But what about his girlfriend? Or your boyfriend?

29 RILEY: I don't know. What should I do?

30 MOLLY: Oh, I'm sorry. We don't offer advice.

31 RILEY: Well then, I'll try to never do it again.

32 MOLLY: I wouldn't. I mean, I would want to, but I'm like
33   you, if he has a girlfriend and you have a boyfriend ...
34   I'd try to never do it again. It wouldn't be right.

35 RILEY: You're right. Thanks. I feel better. *(She exits.)*

1   **MOLLY:** *(To PIPER)* **You're right. This is working. Easy**
2   **money. And those concert tickets will soon be ours to**
3   **have. But I still think we should redo the sign.**
4   **Confessions a dollar. Advice a dollar.**
5   **PIPER: Not a bad idea.** *(Looking ahead)* **Look, Joey**
6   **Leatherwood is heading this way with a dollar in his**
7   **hand.**
8   **MOLLY:** *(Rubbing hands together)* **Oh yeah! Come to me!**
9   *(After PIPER gives her a look)* **I mean, "Come to me,**
10   **money." Not "Come to me, Joey."**
11   **JOEY:** *(Enters.)* **I have a confession.**
12   **MOLLY:** *(Excited)* **Oh, we already know.**
13   **JOEY: You already know my confession?**
14   **MOLLY: I mean, we saw you walking over here and we**
15   **knew you had a confession. That's all I meant.**
16   **PIPER:** *(Takes JOEY's dollar bill.)* **You may now confess your**
17   **sins.**
18   **JOEY: OK. I kissed a girl and she wasn't my girlfriend.**
19   **MOLLY:** *(Excited)* **I know.**
20   **JOEY: You know?**
21   **PIPER: She knows how you feel.** *(Nudges MOLLY.)*
22   **MOLLY: No I don't. I've never kissed a boy.**
23   **PIPER: What she means is she knows the guilt was getting**
24   **to you.**
25   **MOLLY: That's true.**
26   **PIPER: You're forgiven. Please come again.**
27   **JOEY: And you want to know what else?**
28   **MOLLY: I do.**
29   **JOEY: I want to kiss her again.**
30   **MOLLY: And you have a girlfriend and she has a boyfriend.**
31   **How sinfully romantic.**
32   **JOEY: Wait a minute. How do you know all this? Was Riley**
33   **here? Did she confess, too?** *(MOLLY smiles and nods.)*
34   **PIPER: We can't divulge that information. It's strictly**
35   **confidential.**

1 JOEY: Well, what would you do?

2 PIPER: And we don't offer advice either.

3 MOLLY: I know what I would do.

4 PIPER: Molly!

5 JOEY: What? What should I do?

6 PIPER: Molly!

7 MOLLY: Search my heart. Figure out who I liked the best.

8 So would that be your girlfriend or the girl you

9 cheated with?

10 JOEY: I don't know. I'm so confused.

11 PIPER: Well, let me just say this. If you decide to cheat

12 again, please know that we are here for you if you

13 need to make another confession.

14 JOEY: Gee, thanks. I just wish I knew what to do. *(Exits.)*

15 PIPER: I bet he'll be back.

16 MOLLY: *(Dreamily)* I hope so. I'd kiss him.

17 CLAIRE: *(Rushes over.)* My boyfriend was just here and I

18 want to know what he confessed to.

19 PIPER: I'm sorry, but that's strictly confidential.

20 CLAIRE: No! You have to tell me. Because I think he's been

21 cheating on me.

22 MOLLY: You do?

23 CLAIRE: Yes!

24 PIPER: Do you have a confession? It will be one dollar,

25 please.

26 CLAIRE: I don't have a confession, but I need to know if

27 Joey is cheating on me. *(MOLLY nods.)*

28 PIPER: Molly!

29 MOLLY: I didn't say anything.

30 CLAIRE: You nodded!

31 MOLLY: I have a crick in my neck. See? We've been sitting

32 here for so long.

33 CLAIRE: Who is she? Tell me?

34 PIPER: All confessions are strictly confidential.

35 CLAIRE: *(Hands PIPER a dollar.)* I have a confession.

1   PIPER: You may now confess your sins.
2   CLAIRE: I'm going to hurt someone if I'm not told what I
3   need to know. And now! Cafeteria fights do not scare
4   me.
5   PIPER: That would send us all to detention. So please
6   control yourself. Fighting is never a solution.
7   CLAIRE: *(Hands them another dollar.)* Here.
8   PIPER: Another confession?
9   CLAIRE: This is for future sin. Because I will need to
10   confess to starting the blood that's about to spill.
11 MOLLY: *(Blurts out.)* It was Riley! Joey kissed Riley. And he
12   liked it! And she liked it! And now it's all just a big
13   mess. *(Covers her mouth with her hand.)* I can't believe
14   I just said all that.
15 PIPER: Molly!
16 MOLLY: *(To PIPER)* I'm sorry, but I didn't want to get beat
17   up.
18 CLAIRE: I knew it! *(Storms off.)*
19 PIPER: *(Stands.)* Come on. Let's get out of here. I don't
20   want to be around when chairs start flying in the
21   cafeteria.
22 MILLY: Oh, I'd like to watch.
23 PIPER: Come on! Let's go. Confession time is over.
24 MOLLY: *(Following PIPER off, she turns and speaks to the
25   students in the lunchroom.)* To err is human, to
26   forgive is divine!
27 PIPER: Good advice.
28 MOLLY: Thank you.
29 PIPER: Looks like we may be sitting in the cheap seats at
30   that concert. *(MOLLY nods. They exit.)*

12. The Older/Other Woman

CAST: (1M, 4F) ALEX, JENNA, TARA, CAMILLE, LEXI
SETTING: The living room at Alex and Jenna's house

1   *(At rise, ALEX is dancing and singing in the living room.*
2   *JENNA enters.)*
3   **ALEX:** "I wanna rock with you ... all night! Dance with you ...
4   **all night!"**
5   **JENNA:** *(Watching ALEX)* **Really?**
6   **ALEX:** *(Dancing)* **Practicing for tonight. Oh yeah! I've got the**
7   **moves. "I'm gonna rock with you ... all night! Dance**
8   **with you ... all night!"**
9   **JENNA: Are you trying to imitate Michael Jackson? Because**
10   **let me tell you, it's not working.**
11 **ALEX:** *(Ignoring her)* **"I wanna rock with you ... yeah ... all**
12   **night! I wanna rock the night away! I wanna rock with**
13   **you! Yeah! All night! I wanna groove with you! Yeah! All**
14   **night!"**
15 **JENNA: Alex, that's a very bad impression of Michael**
16   **Jackson. He'd be horrified. Are you going to karaoke**
17   **tonight?**
18 **ALEX: Nope. I have a date.**
19 **JENNA: What? My brother has a date?**
20 **ALEX: I do.**
21 **JENNA: With who?**
22 **ALEX: Camille.**
23 **JENNA: Camille with the red glasses and multi-colored**
24   **braces or Camille who drives a corvette to school? No,**
25   **wait. Don't even answer that question.**
26 **ALEX: She's picking me up at seven pm.** *(Short pause)* **In her**
27   **corvette!**
28 **JENNA: No way! She's a senior and you're a nobody**
29   **sophomore.**
30 **ALEX: I guess she likes younger men. And I like older**

1   women! *(Sings.)* "I wanna rock with you ... all night!"

2   JENNA: Are you blackmailing Camille?

3   ALEX: No! Of course not. She came up to me and said,
4   "Hey, you wanna hang out sometime?" And I said,
5   "Sure!"

6   JENNA: Alex, are you sure you didn't dream up this little
7   story of yours? Because the Camille I know who
8   drives a yellow corvette wouldn't be caught dead
9   dating a sophomore.

10   ALEX: Maybe not *any* sophomore, but maybe one who has
11   the looks, the personality ... and the whole package
12   deal going on here ... Honestly, Jenna, I don't see how
13   you could possibly be surprised by this. Just look at
14   me. Yeah, I've got it going on. That's for sure.
15   *(Doorbell rings. Outside is TARA, JENNA's friend. ALEX*
16   *rushes to the door.)* I'll get it! *(Disappointed)* Oh, it's
17   you.

18   TARA: *(Enters.)* Gee, thanks.

19   JENNA: Tara, he thought you were his date.

20   TARA: Oh, your baby brother has a date? With who? And
21   wait a minute. Why is your date picking you up? Oh,
22   that's right. You don't have a driver's license yet, do
23   you? Oh, does this mean you're dating an older
24   woman?

25   ALEX: You are correct, Tara.

26   TARA: Who is it?

27   JENNA: Camille.

28   TARA: Camille? Camille with the red glasses and multi-
29   colored braces? But she's not older than you.

30   ALEX: Wrong Camille.

31   TARA: Not Camille who drives a yellow corvette.

32   ALEX: Bingo.

33   TARA: No way.

34   JENNA: That's what I said. And I'll believe it when I see it.
35   Or rather, I'll believe it when she shows up.

1　TARA: Alex, you're lying.

2　ALEX: No, I'm not, Tara. I swear it's true.

3　JENNA: Then where is she?

4　ALEX: I'm sure she's on the way.

5　TARA: And where are you taking Camille? Or rather,
6　　　　where is she taking you?

7　ALEX: I think I'm going to suggest we go to Charlie's.
8　　　　Where we can dance the night away. *(Sings and*
9　　　　*dances.)* "I wanna rock with you ... all night! Dance
10　　　　with you ... all night!"

11　TARA: That's a very bad impression of Michael Jackson.
12　　　　And not exactly the way the song goes either.

13　ALEX: Close enough. *(Continues.)* "I wanna rock with you
14　　　　... all night! Dance with you ... all night."

15　TARA: *(To JENNA)* Do you believe this?

16　JENNA: No. I think my brother is delusional. Hey, Alex,
17　　　　what time is it?

18　ALEX: *(Looks at his watch.)* Seven-oh-four p.m.

19　JENNA: Uh-huh ...

20　ALEX: Four minutes late doesn't mean anything.

21　TARA: *(To JENNA)* Why would he make something like this
22　　　　up? To impress us? Camille is like the supermodel of
23　　　　Regan High. She does not date sophomores. In fact, I
24　　　　heard she's dating a guy in college.

25　JENNA: I'm telling you, my brother is delusional.

26　ALEX: Hey! She's going to be here. She asked me out and I
27　　　　accepted. What can I say if I'm a couple years
28　　　　younger than Camille? She's attracted to me ... I'm
29　　　　attracted to her ... And unlike some girls, she can see
30　　　　past the age barrier. End of story. "I'm gonna rock
31　　　　with you ... all night! Dance with you ... all night!"

32　JENNA: I think the end of the story will be you getting
33　　　　stood up.

34　TARA: Yep. Poor guy.

35　ALEX: She'll be here. You'll see.

1   JENNA: Hey, Alex. What time is it?

2   ALEX: It's time for you two girls to go away. Skedaddle.

3   JENNA: I'm not going anywhere. I've got to see this for
4   myself. Or see what doesn't happen for myself.

5   TARA: And I'm here to watch with you, girlfriend.

6   JENNA: So, what shall we do while we wait? Possibly for a
7   long time.

8   TARA: Alex, you could entertain us with some more
9   singing and dancing.

10 JENNA: Yeah! And Tara and I will be your judges. *(In a*
11   *British accent)* "That was bloody awful."

12 TARA: "Out of all the people I've seen today, I'm sorry, you
13   have been the worst. Dude, you have no talent."

14 JENNA: "A couple of the notes sounded OK, but you need
15   to face the truth. You, Alex, have no talent. This
16   competition isn't for you."

17 ALEX: Can you two just go away? *(The doorbell rings.)* I'll
18   get it!

19 JENNA: *(Beats him to the door.)* No, I'll get it. *(At the door, to*
20   *TARA)* It's probably Jess. She said she'd drop by later
21   to hang out with us. *(Opens door. Surprised)* Camille!

22 CAMILLE: *(Enters.)* Hi, Jenna. *(Sees TARA.)* Hi, Tara.

23 JENNA: Hi, Camille. Come on in.

24 TARA: I can't believe this.

25 CAMILLE: *(Sees ALEX and smiles.)* Hi, Alex.

26 ALEX: *(Almost singing)* Hel-lo, Camille.

27 CAMILLE: Alex, I was going to ask how you felt about
28   dancing tonight.

29 ALEX: *(He can't believe this.)* How do I feel about dancing?

30 JENNA: *(To CAMILLE)* Would you believe he's been
31   practicing?

32 CAMILLE: Practicing?

33 ALEX: Oh, I dance all the time. It's just my second nature.
34   And yes, I'd love to go out dancing with you.

35 CAMILLE: Perfect.

1   **TARA:** *(To CAMILLE)* **And you want to go out dancing with**
2   **Alex?**
3   **CAMILLE: Yes. Alex is so sweet.**
4   **ALEX:** *(Smiling)* **I'm sweet.**
5   **CAMILLE: And I can't wait for you to meet my little sister.**
6   **ALEX: Your sister?**
7   **CAMILLE: Yes. Lexi. She's in the ninth grade so you**
8   **probably don't know her. She'll be in high school next**
9   **year. She's outside in my car if you want to meet her.**
10 **ALEX: She's coming with us?**
11 **CAMILLE: Yes. I want to introduce the two of you. I think**
12   **you'll be a perfect match.** *(Laughs.)* **Call me "The**
13   **Matchmaker!"**
14 **ALEX: What?**
15 **TARA: Oh, of course. Playing matchmaker for your little**
16   **sister.**
17 **JENNA: Now it makes sense.**
18 **CAMILLE:** *(To ALEX)* **You don't mind, do you?**
19 **ALEX: But I thought ...**
20 **CAMILLE: Lexi has had such bad luck with the boys in her**
21   **middle school. They are all so immature. So, I**
22   **promised to pick out a nice guy from high school ...**
23   **who was fairly close to her age ... that I thought she'd**
24   **like and I could set her up with. I guess you could call**
25   **it a blind date.**
26 **ALEX: But I thought ...**
27 **CAMILLE: Don't be mad at me, Alex. Please.**
28 **ALEX: But you left the blind date part out when you asked**
29   **me to hang out with you.**
30 **CAMILLE: I'm sorry. I didn't want to scare you off. Have I**
31   **scared you off? Please don't be mad at me. It was a**
32   **surprise! And you'll love my little sister, Lexi. I thought**
33   **we'd all go to Charlie's and dance the night away.** *(To*
34   *JENNA and TARA)* **Do you want to come with us?**
35 **TARA: Sounds fun to me.**
36 **JENNA: I'm in.**

1   **CAMILLE: Great!**

2   **ALEX: You know, I'm not so sure about this anymore.**

3   **JENNA: Alex.**

4   **TARA: Come on Alex. It'll be fun!**

5   **CAMILLE: Oh, please. I don't want to disappoint Lexi.**

6   **ALEX: Honestly, Camille, I thought this get-together was**

7   **about me and you. Not me and you and your kid sister**

8   **who's still in middle school. Whom I've never met**

9   **and not sure I want to.**

10 **CAMILLE: Oh, Alex, I'm sorry. But I promise, cross my**

11   **heart, you will like Lexi.**

12 **ALEX: I don't think so, Camille.** *(There is a knock at the*

13   *door. JENNA answers it. LEXI enters.)*

14 **CAMILLE: Hey, Lexi. I was just on my way outside.**

15 **LEXI: Are we going?**

16 **CAMILLE: Well, I'm not sure ...**

17 **ALEX:** *(Seeing LEXI)* **Wow!**

18 **CAMILLE:** *(Smiling at ALEX)* **Wow?**

19 **ALEX: Wow!**

20 **LEXI: So are we going?**

21 **ALEX: Yes we are! We are going dancing.**

22 **CAMILLE: Great.**

23 **TARA: Hey Alex, you can ride with us if you want to.**

24 **LEXI: Can I ride with you, too?**

25 **ALEX: Of course you can.**

26 **CAMILLE: Perfect. Jenna, do you want to ride with me in**

27   **the corvette?**

28 **JENNA: Yes! I'd love to.**

29 **CAMILLE: Great. Let's go.** *(They ALL start out.)*

30 **ALEX: Hey, I'll be right there.**

31 **JENNA: OK. Hurry.**

32 **ALEX:** *(The others exit. Takes a deep breath and smiles.)* **Yes!**

33   *(Sings and dances.)* **"I'm gonna rock with you ... all**

34   **night! Dance with you ... all night!"** *(He rushes out the*

35   *door.)*

13. Crazy Hair Day

CAST: (1M, 3F) ALLISON, MISCHA, SALINA, JOEY
PROPS: Bows, ribbons, or other crazy hair decorations
SETTING: Outside school

1 *(At rise, ALLISON and MISCHA are standing outside the*
2 *school. They have both made their hair look crazy and*
3 *messy with various bows, ribbons, etc.)*
4 **ALLISON:** *(Flips hair.)* **Do you like?**
5 **MISCHA: I love.** *(Flips hair.)* **Do you like?**
6 **ALLISON: Of course, darling.**
7 **MISCHA: I love crazy hair day.**
8 **ALLISON: It beats last week when we had crazy sock day.**
9 **Almost everyone wore colored toe socks.**
10 **MISCHA: And crazy hat day wasn't all that exciting because**
11 **most of the boys wore ball caps.**
12 **ALLISON: Except for Randy. He wore that tall red and white**
13 **hat from Dr. Seuss's** *Cat in the Hat.*
14 **MISCHA: That was good. But other than that, it was a rather**
15 **boring hat day. Straw hats, ball caps, a sombrero, a few**
16 **Santa hats ...**
17 **ALLISON: But look at us. We've got the crazy hair going on.**
18 **MISCHA: Everyone is sure to notice us.**
19 **ALLISON: And Mischa, I think it's very possible that one of**
20 **us will win the spirit award for having the craziest hair.**
21 **MISCHA: I agree.** *(Looks at watch.)* **The bell should be**
22 **ringing soon. Let's head inside.**
23 **ALLISON:** *(As they are walking toward the front door, she*
24 *stops and grabs MISCHA's arm.)* **Hey, Mischa ...**
25 **MISCHA: Yeah?**
26 **ALLISON: Look who is standing at the door staring at us.**
27 **MISCHA: Joey Higginbotham.**
28 **ALLISON: Maybe he thinks we're all that with our crazy**
29 **hair.**

1 MISCHA: Wow, Allison. With Joey staring at us, we may get
2   this kind of reaction all day.
3 ALLISON: Lots of attention. I can handle that.
4 MISCHA: Let's go say hello.
5 SALINA: *(Rushes over.)* Allison! Mischa! What's up with the
6   hair?
7 ALLISON: Cute, huh?
8 MISCHA: Would you say fun and adorable?
9 SALINA: Seriously?
10 MISCHA: Allison and I are both hoping to win the spirit
11   award. Whose hair do you think is the best?
12 SALINA: The best? Don't you mean the worst?
13 ALLISON: I guess we should say the craziest.
14 SALINA: Then you would both get the craziest ... worst hair
15   day award.
16 ALLISON: Mischa, I think it's going to be a tie between the
17   two of us.
18 MISCHA: I think you're right.
19 SALINA: A tie to see who gets the most laughs and people
20   pointing at them?
21 MISCHA: Laughs? *(Flips hair.)* Why would our friends
22   laugh?
23 ALLISON: Joey Higginbotham isn't laughing.
24 MISCHA: Yeah. He's staring at us 'cause he thinks we're all
25   that.
26 SALINA: I'm sorry, but what is this?
27 ALLISON: Mischa, apparently Salina did not get the
28   memo.
29 MISCHA: I think you are right, Allison. Why else would she
30   not show some spirit on crazy hair day?
31 SALINA: Crazy hair day?
32 MISCHA: What other day do you make your hair look
33   crazy?
34 ALLISON: And fun and cute!
35 MISCHA: And did I say adorable?

1   ALLISON: And get the chance to win the spirit award.

2   MISCHA: And a photo op for the school paper.

3   ALLISON: And the yearbook.

4   MISCHA: And stand on the sidelines on Friday night's
5   game.

6   ALLISON: And we've got the spirit. Right here!

7   MISCHA: Yes we do! And Joey Higginbotham seems to be
8   appreciating our spirit. He is like so staring at us.

9   ALLISON: And Joey's on the football team so maybe one of
10   us will be standing on the sidelines with him.
11   *(Waves.)* **Hey, Joey!**

12 MISCHA: *(Waves.)* **Hey, Joey!** I wonder why he didn't wave
13   back?

14 ALLISON: He looks confused.

15 MISCHA: He's probably confused about which one of us
16   has the craziest hair. Eeny, meeny, miny, moe ... I pick
17   ... Me!

18 ALLISON: No, me! *(They share a laugh.)*

19 SALINA: You know what's sad?

20 MISCHA: What? That you forgot it's crazy hair day?

21 ALLISON: And you don't have a chance in the world to win
22   the spirit award?

23 SALINA: No. What's sad is that you two didn't get the
24   memo.

25 MISCHA: What memo?

26 ALLISON: Yeah, what memo?

27 SALINA: Crazy hair day is next week.

28 MISCHA: What?

29 ALLISON: Next week? Seriously?

30 SALINA: Yes! So Joey Higginbotham is staring at you two
31   because you came to school looking like ... like this?

32 ALLISON: But it's Friday! Crazy days are the same days as
33   the football games.

34 SALINA: And the boys wear their football jerseys to school
35   on Fridays, don't they?

1   **ALLISON: Yes.**

2   **SALINA: And is Joey wearing his jersey today?**

3   **ALLISON: No. I wonder why?**

4   **MISCHA: This isn't Friday?**

5   **ALLISON: What day is it? Thursday? But that's not right. I**

6   **have dance lessons on Thursday and I went to that**

7   **yesterday.**

8   **SALINA: It is Friday.**

9   **MISCHA: Then what happened? Crazy hair day was the**

10   **next crazy day on the schedule.**

11   **SALINA: It's the open week.**

12   **ALLISON: You mean this is the week the team is off? They**

13   **don't play?**

14   **SALINA: That's right. Crazy nothing week. No pep rally.**

15   **Normal bell schedule. No cheerleaders running**

16   **through the halls revving up the students.**

17   **MISCHA: No wonder Joey Higginbotham is staring at us.**

18   **He thinks we joined the freaky club.**

19   **ALLISON: This is great. I wish I could go home, but I can't.**

20   **The bus drops me off and picks me up.**

21   **MISCHA: You and me both.**

22   **SALINA: I'd be embarrassed.**

23   **ALLISON: We are, Salina.**

24   **SALINA: Well, have a good day. See ya.** *(Exits.)*

25   **ALLISON: Mischa, I want to crawl underneath a rock.**

26   **MISCHA: I want to join you.**

27   **ALLISON: Look at us! A few minutes ago we thought we**

28   **were the bomb. Now I completely and totally want to**

29   **evaporate.**

30   **MISCHA: It'd take me a long time to get all this stuff out of**

31   **my hair, plus un-rat it and make it look nice and**

32   **straight.**

33   **ALLISON: Me too. This morning I spent two hours on my**

34   **hair. And that's to make it not look good.**

35   **MISCHA: Allison, what are we going to do?**

1 ALLISON: Walk through the halls looking like idiots?

2 MISCHA: I wish I had a paper sack to put over my head.

3 ALLISON: Me too. I could throw it on my head, then cut

4   out little eyes so I could see my assignments on the

5   board. But I don't think Mr. Velasquez will let us do

6   that.

7 MISCHA: He wouldn't. Allison, I'm afraid that after today,

8   our social life will be doomed.

9 ALLISON: I'm afraid you're right.

10 JOEY: *(Enters.)* Hey.

11 MISCHA: Hey, Joey.

12 ALLISON: Hey.

13 JOEY: I was just wondering ... why?

14 MISCHA: Crazy hair day.

15 JOEY: That's next week.

16 ALLISON: It is?

17 JOEY: Yes.

18 ALLISON: Well, silly us.

19 JOEY: Well, it looks crazy.

20 MISCHA: That's the point. Crazy hair day!

21 ALLISON: Crazy, crazy, crazy. That's us!

22 JOEY: *(Shrugs.)* Well, it looks cool.

23 ALLISON: It does?

24 JOEY: Yeah. I like it. See ya around. *(Exits.)*

25 MISCHA: We look cool?

26 ALLISON: Did you hear that? Joey liked it!

27 MISCHA: Then maybe everyone else will like it, too.

28 ALLISON: And we can act like we did our hair like this on

29   purpose.

30 MISCHA: We did, Allison.

31 ALLISON: I mean, on purpose without it being crazy hair

32   day.

33 MISCHA: Good idea.

34 ALLISON: We're starting a new trend. Crazy hair day

35   everyday.

1   MISCHA: Sounds better than not getting the memo.

2   ALLISON: For sure. Come on. Let's go inside and face the

3   world.

4   MISCHA: OK. But you know what?

5   ALLISON: What?

6   MISCHA: I'm still feeling embarrassed about this whole

7   crazy hair on a non-crazy day.

8   ALLISON: I'm with you. But I'm going to fake it.

9   MISCHA: Faking it with an attitude.

10   ALLISON: *(As they start off)* Hello, world! Here we come!

11   MISCHA: Crazy hair and all!

14. Flavor of the Week

CAST: (2F) LINDA, ALLIE
PROPS: Menu, cup, spoon
SETTING: Ice cream parlor

1   *(At rise, LINDA is standing behind the counter, ready to*
2   *take ALLIE's order.)*
3   **LINDA: May I take your order?**
4   **ALLIE: Do you have a menu? I'd like to see a list of all the**
5   **flavors.**
6   **LINDA: Of course.** *(Hands her a menu.)* **Here you go.**
7   **ALLIE:** *(Looking at the menu)* **This is it?**
8   **LINDA: Is there a problem?**
9   **ALLIE: Only three flavors?**
10   **LINDA: Three flavors and a weekly special.**
11   **ALLIE: Most ice cream parlors have at least fifty flavors. You**
12   **have three.**
13   **LINDA: Don't forget the weekly special! This week's special**
14   **is chicken pot pie.**
15   **ALLIE: Chicken pot pie ice cream?**
16   **LINDA: With sprinkles.**
17   **ALLIE: Ooooh! Nasty.**
18   **LINDA: Hey, don't knock it till you try it. Would you care for**
19   **a sample?**
20   **ALLIE: No! I would not. You know, I can't believe you only**
21   **have three flavors of ice cream here.**
22   **LINDA: Well, we are not just any other ice cream parlor.**
23   **ALLIE: I can see that.**
24   **LINDA: Have you decided? Vanilla, chocolate, or strawberry?**
25   **ALLIE: I wanted butter pecan. Or rocky road.**
26   **LINDA: Not on the menu.**
27   **ALLIE: So this is it?**
28   **LINDA: Yes. Vanilla, chocolate, or strawberry. But I tell you**
29   **what I can do. A swirl. Two flavors swirled together.**

1   Now that changes the options, doesn't it? Chocolate
2   and strawberry. Or vanilla and chocolate. Or
3   chocolate and strawberry. Or strawberry and vanilla.
4   Or if you're game, I could swirl in a little flavor of the
5   week. Chicken pot pie and chocolate. Yum! And
6   sprinkles on top. Free of charge.
7 ALLIE: Sherbet?
8 LINDA: Not on the menu.
9 ALLIE: Milkshakes?
10 LINDA: No. Sorry.
11 ALLIE: Smoothies?
12 LINDA: Not that either.
13 ALLIE: Banana split?
14 LINDA: I don't have bananas. Sorry. They turn mushy so
15   quickly. But if you'd like a scoop of each flavor, you
16   can pretend.
17 ALLIE: With whipped cream and cherries on top?
18 LINDA: Sorry, I don't carry whipped cream or cherries.
19   But I do have sprinkles. And those are free of charge.
20 ALLIE: No. I want butter pecan. Or rocky road. Or even
21   cookies and cream. Or how about chocolate chip?
22 LINDA: Vanilla, chocolate, or strawberry? Oh wait! I forgot.
23   I'm out of chocolate. So it's either vanilla or
24   strawberry. No, wait. The strawberry is not quite
25   finished. Freezing as we speak. So that leaves you with
26   vanilla. Would you like sprinkles? Free of charge.
27 ALLIE: Vanilla?
28 LINDA: With sprinkles. OK, so vanilla it is! Did you say you
29   wanted sprinkles?
30 ALLIE: If I'm stuck with vanilla then I want it with
31   chocolate syrup. Lots of chocolate syrup, please.
32 LINDA: I'm sorry, but I don't carry chocolate syrup. And
33   pardon me for pointing this out, but my ice cream
34   does not need to be drowned in gooey artificial
35   flavors.

1 ALLIE: But that's the way I like to eat vanilla ice cream. By
2   itself, it's just too plain.
3 LINDA: Again, I don't have chocolate syrup. Sorry.
4 ALLIE: Whatever happened to *have it your way?*
5 LINDA: That's Burger King. Down the street on Fifth and
6   Maple.
7 ALLIE: What kind of ice cream parlor is this?
8 LINDA: The kind that specializes in the three basic
9   flavors. Vanilla, chocolate, and strawberry. With one
10   exciting flavor of the week. This week's special is
11   chicken pot pie.
12 ALLIE: You already told me that and it sounds completely
13   disgusting. *(Looks at watch.)* This is great. I only have
14   ten more minutes left on my break and I was really
15   craving ice cream. And you're telling me my only
16   option is vanilla.
17 LINDA: With sprinkles.
18 ALLIE: Or chicken pot pie ice cream. And how totally
19   nauseating is that.
20 LINDA: Oh, wait. You know what?
21 ALLIE: What?
22 LINDA: I may have some of last week's flavor of the week
23   leftover. In fact, I know that I do.
24 ALLIE: I'm afraid to ask, but what was last week's flavor?
25 LINDA: Liver and onions!
26 ALLIE: Liver and onions ice cream? Are you serious?
27 LINDA: Yes! I have some in the back. It wasn't one of our
28   most popular flavors. And I don't know why because
29   I think it's to die for. But I think you would like it.
30   And I can put some sprinkles on it for you.
31 ALLIE: No. Absolutely not.
32 LINDA: I'll be right back. You'll love it. *(Exits.)*
33 ALLIE: *(Hollers.)* Don't waste your time! There's no way
34   I'm eating liver and onions ice cream. I don't even
35   like liver and onions when it's prepared in a kitchen.

1   If my mother had ever forced me to eat it, I would

2   have run away from home.

3 **LINDA:** *(From Off-Stage)* You'll love it. I promise.

4 **ALLIE:** I'm not eating it.

5 **LINDA:** *(From Off-Stage)* It's all natural. No artificial

6   flavors.

7 **ALLIE:** Like that would make a difference.

8 **LINDA:** *(From Off-Stage)* With chunks of liver and onions

9   swirled into the ice cream.

10 **ALLIE:** I think I'm going to vomit.

11 **LINDA:** *(From Off-Stage)* Liver, onions, milk, eggs, sugar,

12   vanilla ...

13 **ALLIE:** Barf!

14 **LINDA:** *(From Off-Stage)* I'll be right there.

15 **ALLIE:** Don't waste your time. I'd gag if I took one bite. *(To

16   herself)* Liver and onions ice cream? Who ever heard

17   of such a thing? *(Looking around)* No wonder there

18   are no other customers in here.

19 **LINDA:** *(Enters with a cup and spoon.)* Sprinkles?

20 **ALLIE:** No!

21 **LINDA:** You like it straight up, huh? Here you go.

22 **ALLIE:** *(Takes the cup.)* This looks horrible! *(Smells the ice

23   cream.)* Hmmmm. Surprisingly it doesn't smell all

24   that bad.

25 **LINDA:** It's wonderful. You'll love it.

26 **ALLIE:** No. I can't.

27 **LINDA:** It's on the house.

28 **ALLIE:** That's because you couldn't sell it to anyone else.

29   No one wants to eat liver and onions ice cream.

30 **LINDA:** It just needs to catch on. Once you try it ... Oh,

31   please! Just take one bite. Please.

32 **ALLIE:** All right. I'll take an itty-bitty bite to prove to you

33   that no one in their right mind would ever like it.

34 **LINDA:** Sprinkles?

35 **ALLIE:** No! *(Takes a bite. Pause)*

1   **LINDA: Well?**

2   **ALLIE:** *(Takes another bite.)* **Did you make up this recipe**

3   **yourself?**

4   **LINDA: I did. My specialty. I just wish it would catch on.**

5   **ALLIE:** *(Takes another bite.)* **This is actually good.**

6   **LINDA: I knew it! I knew you'd like it!**

7   **ALLIE:** *(Another bite)* **It's good. It's really good.** *(Holds out*

8   *the cup.)* **Can I have sprinkles?**

9   **LINDA: Of course.**

15. Lampshade Head

CAST: (3M, 5F) BEN, AMBER, ELLIE, MATT, DAVE, MRS.
  FABER, MRS. JONES, MRS. LIVELY
PROPS: Lampshade
SETTING: Corner of a school hallway

1   *(At rise, BEN stands On-Stage with a lampshade on his*
2   *head.)*
3 **AMBER:** *(Enters. Approaches BEN and stares at him for a*
4   *moment.)* **Weird.** *(Exits.)*
5 **ELLIE:** *(Enters. Approaches BEN and stops.)* **Hello? Hello?**
6   *(Silence. She knocks on the lampshade.)*
7 **BEN: Yes?**
8 **ELLIE: Are you there?**
9 **BEN: I am.**
10 **ELLIE: Can we talk?**
11 **BEN: I'm listening.**
12 **ELLIE: I'm sorry.**
13 **BEN: For what?**
14 **ELLIE: For what I said.**
15 **BEN: Which was?**
16 **ELLIE: I said you weren't very bright.** *(Pause)* **Did you hear**
17   **me?** *(Knocks on lampshade.)* **I said I was sorry.**
18 **BEN: I heard you.**
19 **ELLIE: And I only said you weren't very bright because you**
20   **keep putting your sheet music in *my* band locker.**
21 **BEN: Our lockers are next to each other. I get mixed up.**
22 **ELLIE: I'm locker twenty-six.**
23 **BEN: And I'm locker seventy-one.**
24 **ELLIE: Miles apart! And my locker is decorated with pink**
25   **zebra paper with my name arched in hot pink letters.**
26   ***Ellie.* How is that confusing?**
27 **BEN: I'm blind?**
28 **ELLIE: Well, your *Drunken Sailor* and *Greensleeves* sheet**

1   music keeps getting thrown into my locker. Along
2   with your trombone mouthpiece. Are you in such a
3   hurry to get out of band that you just throw your
4   stuff in the closest locker?
5 BEN: I was confused.
6 ELLIE: Well, anyway ... I'm sorry for embarrassing you in
7   class today. I'm sorry the whole class saw me having
8   a slight meltdown when I pulled your trombone
9   music out of my locker for the fourth time this week.
10   And I'm sorry for screaming and stomping on your
11   papers. And I'm sorry Mr. Peterson had to call you to
12   the front of the class to lecture you about getting
13   your head out of your ... well ... wherever he said your
14   head was. And I'm sorry he forced you to practice
15   putting your sheet music in your own locker over and
16   over again while the rest of the class played music.
17 BEN: Laughing stock of the class.
18 ELLIE: I just don't like other people getting into my
19   locker. Especially boys. And especially someone who
20   leaves a nasty slobbery trombone mouthpiece all
21   over my *Ave Maria* music!
22 BEN: I'm an idiot.
23 ELLIE: I said you weren't bright because you weren't
24   acting very bright.
25 BEN: I'm acting bright now.
26 ELLIE: Well, whatever. *(Exits.)*
27 AMBER: *(Enters. Approaches BEN and stops.)* Are you
28   drunk? *(Exits.)*
29 MATT: *(Enters.)* Some starting pitcher you are. Trying to
30   hide? I would.
31 BEN: Coach Davis hates me.
32 MATT: You lost the game for us. Walked fourteen batters.
33 BEN: I couldn't find the strike zone.
34 MATT: Couldn't find the strike zone? That's an
35   understatement. You threw wild pitches, gave up

1   home runs, walked batters, and beaned a few guys on
2   top of that! Way to go, pitcher.

3 BEN: I guess I didn't bring my best to the field.

4 MATT: Duh! We lost. Lost big time. Wildcats ten. Mustangs
5   zero! Way to go, pitcher. Turn out the lights, the
6   party's over. *(He exits.)*

7 AMBER: *(Enters. Approaches BEN and stops.)* Are you
8   pretending to be a standing lamp?

9 BEN: Maybe.

10 AMBER: Well, it's totally dumb and immature.

11 BEN: I know.

12 AMBER: I think you are drunk.

13 BEN: No.

14 AMBER: Yes. Because I've heard that drunk people put
15   lampshades on their head. I'm not sure why. Unless they
16   think it's their hat. Is that your hat or are you a lamp?

17 BEN: I don't know.

18 AMBER: You're weird. *(Exits.)*

19 BEN: Thank you.

20 DAVE: *(Enters. Laughing)* Ben! You're turning into the class
21   clown.

22 BEN: How'd you know it was me?

23 DAVE: I'd recognize you anywhere. I heard about the
24   prank you pulled on Mrs. Faber.

25 BEN: Which prank?

26 DAVE: Which prank? Man, you crack me up. You did all
27   those pranks?

28 BEN: Maybe.

29 DAVE: Gluing Mrs. Faber's computer mouse to the desk
30   with superglue?

31 BEN: Guilty.

32 DAVE: The goldfish in her water bottle?

33 BEN: Guilty.

34 DAVE: Shining the laser pointer on her backside when she
35   turned around?

1   **BEN:** Guilty.

2   **DAVE:** Sardines in the air vent?

3   **BEN:** Guilty.

4   **DAVE:** Ah, man! You are officially the class clown. And

5   what's up with the lampshade? Another joke you're

6   pulling on someone?

7   **BEN:** Maybe.

8   **DAVE:** Man, you've got guts. I'd be too afraid to get caught.

9   Has Mrs. Faber figured out it was you pulling all the

10   pranks in her class?

11 **BEN:** Not yet.

12 **DAVE:** Well, let's hope she doesn't. 'Cause if she does you

13   are going to detention.

14 **BEN:** I know.

15 **DAVE:** Then the fun and games will be over. Mrs.

16   Snodgrass, who's in charge of detention, is a mean

17   and hard woman. She sticks you in a room with no

18   windows and you enter at your own risk. No smiles.

19   No second chances. No rewards or pats on the back.

20   It's all glares and assignments. Talk about not feeling

21   the love.

22 **BEN:** You been?

23 **DAVE:** No, but I've heard about it. And believe me, you

24   don't want to go there. Well, see ya.

25 **BEN:** See ya. *(DAVE exits. MRS. FABER and MRS. JONES*

26   *enter. They stand by BEN but do not notice him.)*

27 **MRS. FABER:** If I could find the prankster who keeps

28   messing with my classroom ...

29 **MRS. JONES:** Oh, you have one of those this year?

30 **MRS. FABER:** Yes. And I'm about ready to squeeze the

31   living life out of this person.

32 **MRS. JONES:** No tattletales?

33 **MRS FABER:** Are you kidding? The class loves the pranks.

34   One day I drank half my bottled water before I

35   noticed a goldfish swimming in it.

1 MRS. JONES: Oh my! I once found goldfish in the teachers'
2   bathroom.
3 MRS. FABER: What did you do?
4 MRS. JONES: Flushed them.
5 MRS. FABER: And this little prankster super-glued my
6   mouse to the desk.
7 MRS. JONES: Oh, that would irritate me. And not one
8   tattletale in the classroom?
9 MRS. FABER: No! I've even offered a cash reward for
10   information leading to the capture of the little devil
11   prankster.
12 MRS. JONES: How much?
13 MRS. FABER: Fifty dollars.
14 MRS. JONES: Are we allowed to do that?
15 MRS. FABER: No one said I couldn't. I even put a sign on
16   the blackboard. "Reward of fifty dollars will be given
17   for any information leading to the capture of the
18   person or persons responsible for pulling pranks in
19   my classroom."
20 MRS. JONES: I'm surprised you haven't received any
21   information. Kids are always in need of a little extra
22   cash.
23 MRS. FABER: I know. And I even offered to keep that
24   person's identity a secret.
25 MRS. JONES: Surely someone will come forward.
26 MRS. FABER: I hope so. Because almost every day in
27   fourth period, I hear laughter every time I turn my
28   back. Someone is doing something.
29 MRS. JONES: Could be a laser pen. I caught a student
30   doing that to me one day. Yanked him up and
31   escorted him straight to Mrs. Snodgrass. Detention
32   for six weeks. He's a very polite and respectful
33   student now.
34 MRS. FABER: Yes, that Mrs. Snodgrass knows how to tame
35   them.

1   **MRS. JONES: Well, let's hope you find your prankster.**

2   **MRS. FABER: Yes.** *(She turns to the lamp and looks at it.*

3   *After a moment, she wipes it with her fingers, and then*

4   *looks at her fingers.)* **Someone needs to dust this**

5   **lampshade.** *(MRS. FABER and MRS. JONES exit.*

6   *AMBER enters. She approaches BEN and stops. A*

7   *pause)*

8   **BEN: Who's there?**

9   **AMBER: Is that the game you want to play? Knock knock?**

10 **BEN: Who's there?**

11 **AMBER: I am.**

12 **BEN: I am who?**

13 **AMBER: You don't know who you are?**

14 **BEN: Not funny.**

15 **AMBER: Yes it was! So, what are you doing under there?**

16 **BEN: Nothing.**

17 **AMBER: Are you trying to draw attention to yourself?**

18 **BEN: Maybe.**

19 **AMBER: Are you hiding from someone?**

20 **BEN: Maybe.**

21 **AMBER: Maybe so, maybe no?**

22 **BEN: Maybe.**

23 **AMBER: I know what it is.**

24 **BEN: What?**

25 **AMBER: You're drunk!** *(She exits.)*

26 **MRS. LIVELY:** *(Enters.)* **Look at you! I love it!**

27 **BEN: You love it?**

28 **MRS. LIVELY: Yes! Are you in my class?**

29 **BEN: No.**

30 **MRS. LIVELY: I didn't think so. Well, you should be.**

31 **BEN: I should?**

32 **MRS. LIVELY: Yes! Students who thrive on attention**

33   **should be in my class. And you, standing here with a**

34   **lampshade on your head, tells me you love attention.**

35   **Is that right, Mr. Lampshade Head?**

1   **BEN: Maybe.**

2   **MRS. LIVELY: And I bet you are a fine actor, too.**

3   **BEN: I'm not sure.**

4   **MRS. LIVELY: Try this. "To be, or not to be; that is the**

5   **question."**

6   **BEN: Shakespeare.**

7   **MRS. LIVELY: Very good. Come on. Let me hear you! Try it.**

8   **BEN:** *(Dramatically)* **To be, or not to be, that is the question,**

9   **whether 'tis nobler in the mind to suffer, the slings**

10   **and arrows of outrageous fortune, or to take arms**

11   **against a sea of troubles ... oh yes, a sea of troubles!**

12   **MRS. LIVELY: Oh yes! You have the gift of acting. Even**

13   **with a lampshade on your head.**

14   **BEN: Thank you.**

15   **MRS. LIVELY: You must try out for the fall play next week.**

16   **We're doing** *Hamlet.* **And a fine Hamlet you would**

17   **make.**

18   **BEN: Me? Hamlet?**

19   **MRS. LIVELY: Yes! One of Shakespeare's most powerful**

20   **and influential tragedies. And if I can find the perfect**

21   **person to play Hamlet, the fall play will be a**

22   **theatrical masterpiece. So tell me, Mr. Lampshade**

23   **Head, will you come to tryouts? Oh please. Please say**

24   **yes!**

25   **BEN: Yes.**

26   **MRS. LIVELY: Wonderful! Oh, how wonderful.** *(As she is*

27   *exiting)* **I believe I have found my Hamlet.**

28   **AMBER:** *(Enters).* **Aren't you tired of being a lamp?**

29   **BEN: "To be, or not to be; that is the question."**

30   **AMBER:** *(As she is exiting)* **Whatever.**

31   **BEN:** *(Removes the lamp shade. Looks around. Then*

32   *dramatically:)* **"To be, or not to be; that is the**

33   **question!"**

16. Prom Date

CAST: (3M, 1F) CALEB, LOGAN, ISAAC, SCARLET
PROPS: Books
SETTING: Library

1　　*(At rise, CALEB, LOGAN, and ISAAC are sitting at a table in*
2　　　　*the library. Further away, SCARLET sits at another table.)*
3　CALEB: Question. If you could ask any girl to the prom,
4　　　　who'd it be?
5　LOGAN: Scarlet Cates.
6　ISAAC: Me too. Scarlet Cates.
7　CALEB: Yeah, Scarlet Cates for me, too.
8　LOGAN: I wonder who she's going with?
9　ISAAC: Maybe no one. She and Rusty broke up last week.
10　LOGAN: So do you think she needs a date?
11　ISAAC: Nah. I'm sure she can pick any guy she wants.
12　LOGAN: Pick me!
13　ISAAC: No, me!
14　CALEB: Question. If you could ask any girl to the prom, that
15　　　　might say yes, who'd it be?
16　LOGAN: That might say yes?
17　ISAAC: That might say yes if she was offered a million
18　　　　dollars to go?
19　LOGAN: Then I'd say Scarlet Cates.
20　ISAAC: Me too. Scarlet Cates. Here, take this million dollars
21　　　　and make my dream come true.
22　CALEB: So who'd be your second choice?
23　LOGAN: Second choice would be a *Sports Illustrated*
24　　　　swimsuit model.
25　ISAAC: You know any?
26　LOGAN: No. Like how would I know any *SI* models?
27　ISAAC: I don't know. Just asking.
28　CALEB: Well, I think one of us should ask Scarlet to the
29　　　　prom.

1   **ISAAC: Seriously?**
2   **LOGAN: For a joke?**
3   **ISAAC: Not me.**
4   **LOGAN: Me neither. I have a fear of rejection.**
5   **ISAAC: I've already had my share of nos. Three to be exact.**
6   **Three days, three nos. Sophie said, "I'm sorry, Isaac,**
7   **but I already have a date." Megan laughed at me so I**
8   **took that as a no. Tamara said, "No, I don't believe I'd**
9   **like to go with you, but thank you for asking." Like I**
10   **said, three days, three nos. I'm over it.**
11 **LOGAN: I haven't even asked one girl to the prom. I'm still**
12   **afraid of girls, remember? They come near me and I**
13   **become tongue-tied and fidget nervously. I would be**
14   **like, "I ... I ... I ... uh ...uh ... Scarlet ... I ... uh ... see I ... uh**
15   **... would you ... I mean, I know you wouldn't, but I ...**
16   **uh ... uh ... wondered ... don't wonder ... know you**
17   **wouldn't ... but hoped ... uh ... wished ... prayed ... uh,**
18   **yes, I ... uh ... really prayed ... uh ... would it help if I**
19   **begged? No? No, I won't beg. I'm stupid. Yes, call me**
20   **stupid. But anyway ... uh ... I was wondering ...**
21   **thinking ... uh ... you wouldn't want to go with me to**
22   **the prom, would you?"**
23 **ISAAC:** *(In a girl's voice)* **I'd love to!**
24 **LOGAN: Right. Like that would happen.**
25 **ISAAC:** *(In a girl's voice)* **Yes, I'd love to go with you, Logan!**
26   **And now I've got to rush off to the mall and find the**
27   **perfect dress. And make an appointment to get my**
28   **hair done. And my nails! And oh, there's only one**
29   **week left to do it all.** *(Jumps up and down.)* **I'm so**
30   **excited! Just so excited! I'm going to the prom with**
31   **Logan!** *(The BOYS laugh.)*
32 **LOGAN: I say we hit up the court and play some basketball**
33   **on prom night.**
34 **ISAAC: I'm in.**
35 **LOGAN: You in too, Caleb?**

1 CALEB: No, I'm going to the prom.
2 ISAAC: With who? Scarlet Cates? *(The BOYS laugh.)*
3 CALEB: Maybe. She could say yes.
4 LOGAN: Sure she could.
5 ISAAC: Sure. Anything is possible.
6 LOGAN: Yeah, like a one-in-trillion chance of getting hit
7   by a meteorite too. So sure, it's always possible.
8 CALEB: I'm sure Scarlet needs a date to the prom since
9   she and Rusty broke up. And what guy would dare to
10   make him jealous? He's got arms of steel. He could
11   crush any guy with a single-handed snap.
12 LOGAN: Which means you've got guts if you plan to ask
13   Scarlet out.
14 ISAAC: Yeah, 'cause you know Rusty wants her back.
15 LOGAN: I heard him telling Josh Rivera that he was going
16   to wait until the day before the prom and let her
17   know he'd take her back.
18 ISAAC: So there you go. Rusty and Scarlet will be going to
19   the prom together after all.
20 CALEB: Not necessarily. She might decide to go with
21   someone else.
22 ISAAC: With who?
23 LOGAN: You?
24 CALEB: I'm not a bad looking guy, am I?
25 LOGAN: Don't ask me.
26 ISAAC: I have no opinion.
27 CALEB: Well, I say I'm just as desirable as the next guy.
28 ISAAC: I've heard that attitude is everything.
29 CALEB: *(Looks toward SCARLET.)* So I'll just walk over
30   there and ask if she wants to go with me to the prom.
31 ISAAC: Good luck with that.
32 LOGAN: And if she says no?
33 CALEB: Who says she's going to say no?
34 ISAAC: I say if she says no … well, at least you tried.
35 LOGAN: Because quitters don't win. Or something like
36   that.

1   ISAAC: Yeah. If at first you don't succeed, try, try, again.

2   Well, maybe not. If she says no, just smile and tell her

3   it was a joke. A dare. Yeah, a dare! Tell her that you

4   really didn't want to go with her in the first place, but

5   you had to follow through on a dare to show you

6   weren't a coward.

7   LOGAN: Good idea, Isaac.

8   CALEB: Well, I think Scarlet will say yes.

9   ISAAC: And we like your attitude, don't we, Logan?

10   LOGAN: Yes we do, Isaac. And I say we go sit next to

11   Scarlet's table so we can hear everything that's said.

12   But don't worry, Caleb. We won't say a word. Not a

13   word. We'll just sit there quietly and keep our heads

14   buried in our books.

15   ISAAC: But just talk loud enough so we can hear

16   everything, OK?

17   CALEB: OK. You two head on over there and I'll be there in

18   a minute.

19   ISAAC: Good luck.

20   LOGAN: Yeah, good luck, man. *(ISAAC and LOGAN go sit*

21   *next to SCARLET's table. They both open a book and*

22   *pretend to read.)*

23   CALEB: *(Clears his throat and practices.)* **Will you ... ?** *(Clears*

24   *throat.)* **Would you ... ?** *(Deep breath)* **I'd be honored ...**

25   **No.** *(Deep breath. Then in a nonchalant tone)* **Hey, if**

26   **you don't have any plans for the prom why don't we**

27   **hook up?** *(Shakes head, then walks toward SCARLET.*

28   *He stands by her table, staring at her.)*

29   SCARLET: *(Looks up.)* **Hey.**

30   CALEB: **Hey.**

31   SCARLET: You want to sit down? No one is sitting here.

32   CALEB: Yes. *(Starts to sit.)* **No! I'd rather stand.**

33   SCARLET: *(Gives him a strange look.)* **OK.**

34   CALEB: *(Clears throat.)* **Has anyone ever told you you'd**

35   **make a great *SI* model?**

1   **SCARLET:** *SI?*

2   **CALEB:** *Sports Illustrated.*

3   **SCARLET:** Uh ... no. But thanks. I guess.

4   **CALEB:** You would.

5   **SCARLET:** Thanks.

6   **CALEB:** *(Deep breath, then blurts out quickly)* **Are you**

7   **going to the prom? I mean, I heard you and Rusty**

8   **broke up and I figured you didn't have a date. Maybe**

9   **you need one. I need one. Not that I'm desperate or**

10   **anything. I just thought if you needed a date like I**

11   **needed a date we might go to the prom together. Is**

12   **that stupid or what?** *(ISAAC and LOGAN shake their*

13   *heads and disappear behind their books for a moment.*

14   *Then peek over the books to hear SCARLET's response.)*

15 **SCARLET:** *(Pause as she looks at CALEB)* **Did you just ask**

16   **me to the prom?**

17 **CALEB:** I think so.

18 **SCARLET:** Oh, how sweet of you! And I'd love to go.

19 **CALEB:** *(Excited)* **You would?**

20 **SCARLET:** I would, but ...

21 **CALEB:** But?

22 **SCARLET:** Yes, but I already have a date.

23 **CALEB:** *(Disappointed)* **Oh.**

24 **SCARLET:** I'm taking my little brother. Joey. He's in sixth

25   grade. I thought it'd be fun for him. And yes, I did

26   need a date.

27 **CALEB:** I see.

28 **SCARLET:** But if you want to come along ...

29 **CALEB:** The three of us?

30 **SCARLET:** Well, it's not like I'm going to spend the entire

31   night dancing with my little brother. He doesn't even

32   like to dance. He'll probably hang out at the snack

33   table most of the night. Or take advantage of the

34   tarot reader who will be there. So, what do you say?

35 **CALEB:** Scarlet, are you asking me to the prom?

1   **SCARLET: Yes, if you want to go with me and my little**
2   **brother.**
3   **CALEB: I'd love to!**
4   **SCARLET:** *(Stands.)* **Great.** *(Kisses his cheek.)* **Pick us up at**
5   **seven. OK?**
6   **CALEB: OK!**
7   **SCARLET: Bye.**
8   **CALEB: Bye.** *(SCARLET exits. ISAAC and LOGAN get up and*
9   *join CALEB.)*
10   **ISAAC: No way!**
11   **LOGAN: How'd you do that?**
12   **CALEB: It's my charm. Good looks. My confidence. Great**
13   **personality. What can I say?**
14   **ISAAC: Man, you've got guts.**
15   **LOGAN:** *(To ISAAC)* **And I guess it's gonna be you and me**
16   **on prom night for a little one on one.**
17   **ISAAC:** *(As if shooting a basketball)* **Swish. Right in the**
18   **basket! Yeah!**
19   **LOGAN: Gonna be hard to beat me!** *(As if shooting a*
20   *basketball)* **Swish. Yeah!**
21   **CALEB: And I will be taking the next** *SI* **model to the prom.**
22   **Yeah! Go me!**

17. Big Flirt

CAST: (2M, 2F) KACI, AUSTIN, RYAN, LAUREN
SETTING: The mall

1   KACI: *(Arms crossed)* **We were just talking.**

2   AUSTIN: **About what?**

3   KACI: **Reincarnation.**

4   AUSTIN: **Why? Because you and Jake thought you were in**

5   **love in your previous life?**

6   KACI: **No! It was just random stuff about reincarnation.**

7   AUSTIN: **And maybe next time around you two will hook up?**

8   KACI: **No, Austin! Why do you have to be so jealous all the**

9   **time?**

10 AUSTIN: **Kaci, it's because you make me jealous.**

11 KACI: **How?**

12 AUSTIN: *(Talks like a girl, swings his hips, and touches KACI's*

13   *arm.)* **Oh, you're just so funny! I love your jokes.**

14 KACI: **I don't do that.**

15 AUSTIN: *(Still talking like a girl)* **Do you like my nails? I had**

16   **them painted yesterday. See the little designs? Do you**

17   **like the little hearts?**

18 KACI: **Austin, that's not funny.**

19 AUSTIN: *(Still talking like a girl)* **And do you like my new**

20   **shirt? I found it on sale. I think it's cute. Do you think**

21   **it's cute?**

22 KACI: **Austin, I don't act like that.**

23 AUSTIN: **Yes you do, Kaci. Yesterday you went up to Conner**

24   **... with me standing right there ... and you were like this**

25   **...** *(Flips hair, talks like a girl)* **Conner, you should add me**

26   **as your friend on Facebook!**

27 KACI: **So?**

28 AUSTIN: *(Moving his hips around)* **And you should check out**

29   **my profile. And look at my pictures. That is ...** *(Swings*

       hips) **if you want to. Wink, wink.**

1   KACI: I didn't wink at Conner.

2   AUSTIN: You might as well have. So tell me, did Conner

3   add you as his friend on Facebook?

4   KACI: No. Because I added him first.

5   AUSTIN: Just what you needed! One more boy friend on

6   Facebook.

7   KACI: Hey, I can be friends with boys. You're just insecure.

8   AUSTIN: No, you're just a big flirt, Kaci.

9   KACI: No I'm not! *(Looks away.)* Hey, there's Ryan. Hey,

10   Ryan!

11 RYAN: *(Enters.)* Hey, what's up.

12 KACI: *(Touches his arm.)* Ryan, Austin and I are having a

13   disagreement. Could you possibly be an objective

14   person for us?

15 RYAN: *(Appears to be taken with KACI. Smiling)* I'll try.

16 KACI: *(Swings her hips and flips her hair.)* OK, here's the

17   thing ... *(Touches RYAN's shoulder.)* And Ryan, I want

18   you to be totally honest, OK?

19 RYAN: OK.

20 KACI: Even if it hurts someone's feelings. Not that you

21   would hurt my feelings. *(Touching his arm)* Because

22   you are just so sweet. *(Touches his face.)* And cute.

23   *(Gives him a big smile.)* But that doesn't have anything

24   to do with this. *(Touches his hair.)* And you can't help

25   it if you're cute, can you?

26 RYAN: I guess not.

27 AUSTIN: Uh-huh.

28 KACI: Uh-huh what, Austin?

29 AUSTIN: You've just proven my point, Kaci. You're a big

30   flirt.

31 KACI: How?

32 AUSTIN: *(Reaches over and touches RYAN's face. Talks like a*

33   *girl.)* You're just so cute. But you can't help that, can

34   you?

35 RYAN: Whoa! That's not right.

1   AUSTIN: Just making my point.

2   KACI: That wasn't flirting.

3   AUSTIN: It's not? Ryan, is that not flirting to you?

4   RYAN: I don't know. I'm confused. What's going on here?

5   AUSTIN: Is this flirting to you? *(Reaches over and touches*

6   *RYAN's face. Talks like a girl.)* You're so cute!

7   RYAN: No! No, it's not!

8   KACI: See.

9   AUSTIN: *(To RYAN)* Not me flirting. But is it flirting when

10   Kaci does it?

11   RYAN: I don't know.

12   AUSTIN: Do it again, Kaci.

13   KACI: Do what again?

14   AUSTIN: That "you're so cute" thing.

15   KACI: Why?

16   AUSTIN: Just do it. Humor me.

17   KACI: *(To RYAN, dryly)* You're cute, Ryan.

18   RYAN: O-K.

19   AUSTIN: Not like that! Do it like you did it before. Like

20   this. *(Swings his hips and reaches out for RYAN.)*

21   RYAN: *(Steps back.)* Whoa, dude!

22   AUSTIN: Ryan, I'm just being Kaci.

23   RYAN: *(Looking around)* I'm sorry, but this is just way too

24   uncomfortable for me. If someone saw what you

25   were doing ... whatever your motive is ... well, I can't

26   deal with that. You know?

27   AUSTIN: *(Frustrated)* Kaci, do it again.

28   KACI: *(Reaches out quickly, abruptly)* Ryan, you're cute.

29   RYAN: Thanks. Gosh, I don't know when I've been told

30   how cute I am so many times in one day ... *(Looks at*

31   *AUSTIN.)* And in so many ways.

32   AUSTIN: So Ryan, was that flirting to you?

33   RYAN: *(Looking at AUSTIN)* Were you flirting with me?

34   AUSTIN: Not me. Her.

35   RYAN: Oh! Thank God.

1   AUSTIN: But was Kaci flirting?

2   RYAN: I don't think so.

3   KACI: See.

4   RYAN: *(To AUSTIN)* I mean, no more than you. And you
5   said you weren't flirting with me. Again, thank God!
6   So, I'd just have to say no. Kaci was not flirting with
7   me. So, did I solve the disagreement the two of you
8   were having? I hope so because I've gotta run. Soccer
9   practice in half an hour.

10 KACI: *(Kisses RYAN's cheek.)* Thanks, Ryan. You're a
11   sweetheart!

12 RYAN: Anytime! *(Exits.)*

13 AUSTIN: I can't believe that. You just kissed him!

14 KACI: No, I didn't.

15 AUSTIN: Yes, you did! Right there in front of me.

16 KACI: That was not a kiss. It was just a thank you.

17 AUSTIN: Oh! Oh! So can I thank girls like that?

18 KACI: Uh, no!

19 AUSTIN: Why not?

20 KACI: Because!

21 AUSTIN: Because why? Because if you can go around
22   kissing other boys then I should be able to go around
23   kissing other girls. What's good for you should be
24   good for me. *(LAUREN enters. Immediately, AUSTIN
25   begins flirting with her.)* Lauren! Did I thank you for
26   picking up my history assignments last week when I
27   was out sick?

28 LAUREN: Yes, and you're welcome.

29 AUSTIN: Well, let me thank you properly.

30 LAUREN: Thank you is sufficient.

31 AUSTIN: Lauren ... *(Touches her face.)* You're so pretty.

32 LAUREN: *(Giving him a strange look)* Uh ... thanks.

33 AUSTIN: And thanks again for picking up my assignments
34   for me. *(Kisses LAUREN's cheek.)*

35 LAUREN: *(Pushes him.)* Why did you do that?

1   AUSTIN: I was thanking you.

2   LAUREN: Listen here, Austin, you keep your stinking lips

3   to yourself. Do you hear me? And next time you need

4   someone to pick up your history assignments when

5   you're sick, ask someone else. *(She stomps off.)*

6   KACI: I can't believe you just kissed another girl. And

7   right in front of me!

8   AUSTIN: But I was just trying to prove my point.

9   KACI: We are over. *(She stomps off.)*

10 AUSTIN: *(Throws his hands in the air.)* Girls!

18. A Change of Heart

CAST: (2M) NICK, BRETT
PROPS: Ring box, magnifying glass
SETTING: Brett's bedroom

1   *(At rise, NICK and BRETT are standing in BRETT's*
2   *bedroom. BRETT is holding a ring box.)*
3   **NICK: What do you mean you bought Madison a ring? Like**
4   **an engagement ring?**
5   **BRETT: It's a promise ring.**
6   **NICK: You want to get married?**
7   **BRETT: To Madison? Yes.**
8   **NICK: What has happened to my friend here?**
9   **BRETT: It's love, Nick. Someday it might happen to you.**
10 **NICK: I hope not.**
11 **BRETT:** *(Holds out the ring box.)* **Do you want to see it?**
12 **NICK: Sure. Let me see it.**
13 **BRETT:** *(Opens the box.)* **What do you think?**
14 **NICK: Where's the diamond?**
15 **BRETT: It's in there. It's just really small.**
16 **NICK: I don't see it.**
17 **BRETT:** *(Hands him a magnifying glass.)* **Here. Use this.**
18 **NICK: Oh yeah. Now I see it.**
19 **BRETT: Do you like it?**
20 **NICK: I guess. But I'm not really into rings.**
21 **BRETT: Do you think Madison will like it?**
22 **NICK:** *(Takes the magnifying glass and looks at the ring again.)*
23   **She might be disappointed.**
24 **BRETT: Why?**
25 **NICK: Because girls like big, humongous diamonds. So they**
26   **can show it off to all their girlfriends.**
27 **BRETT: Well, that's all I could afford.**
28 **NICK: Maybe you should offer her the magnifying glass like**
29   **you did to me when you ask her to marry you.**

1   **BRETT: Do you think?**

2   **NICK: She'll want to see the diamond.**

3   **BRETT: Don't you think that takes the romance out of it**

4   **when I have to hand her a magnifying glass after she**

5   **opens the box?**

6   **NICK: Perhaps. But maybe Madison will be so excited to**

7   **get a promise ring from you that the size of the**

8   **diamond won't matter.**

9   **BRETT: I hope so. I'm counting on it. I spent several**

10   **months of allowance on this ring. She has to say yes.**

11   **NICK:** *(Looking at the ring again with the magnifying glass)*

12   **I think she'll like it. As long as you let her look at it**

13   **with this.** *(Hands the magnifying glass back to BRETT.)*

14   **So, are you nervous?**

15   **BRETT: I am. We're having dinner tonight and that's**

16   **when I'm going to pop the question.**

17   **NICK: Wow. Are you sure you're ready for this kind of**

18   **commitment?**

19   **BRETT: Nick, it's not an engagement ring, it's a promise**

20   **ring.**

21   **NICK: Still a commitment.**

22   **BRETT: Well, it's not like we're going to start wedding**

23   **plans. Just promising to love each other forever and**

24   **someday get married.**

25   **NICK: Wow. And you're still in high school.**

26   **BRETT: Doesn't matter.**

27   **NICK: I don't know any other sophomores who are**

28   **engaged. Do you?**

29   **BRETT: Not engaged. Promised.**

30   **NICK: But still ...**

31   **BRETT: Nick, you don't understand. Madison and I love**

32   **each other. We're destined to be together for the rest**

33   **of our lives.**

34   **NICK: The rest of your life is a long time.**

35   **BRETT: Like I said, Madison and I love each other.**

1   **NICK: This week.**

2   **BRETT: What?**

3   **NICK: You know how girls are. They change their minds.**

4   **You're here today, gone tomorrow. One day you are**

5   **the love of her life, the next day she won't speak to**

6   **you in the hallway between classes.**

7   **BRETT: That won't happen with Madison and I.**

8   **NICK: Brett, she is your first *real* girlfriend.**

9   **BRETT: So?**

10   **NICK: So I'm just saying that maybe you need to play the**

11   **field first. See what else is out there.**

12   **BRETT: No! I'm committed to Madison.**

13   **NICK: And what if Tori Welch invited you to her birthday**

14   **bash?**

15   **BRETT: You mean as her date? She wouldn't do that.**

16   **NICK: What if I heard she might?**

17   **BRETT: I'm still committed to Madison. But is that true?**

18   **You heard Tori might ask me to her birthday party?**

19   **NICK: Through the grapevine. But I'll send the**

20   **information back that you are not available.**

21   **Promised to Madison forever. Forever and ever and**

22   **ever! Till death do you part. But you know what? That**

23   **Tori is a babe. That long blonde hair. Big blue eyes ...**

24   **those curves.** *(With his hands, makes a curve gesture.)*

25   **One cute girl!**

26   **BRETT: Tori wouldn't ask me to her party.**

27   **NICK.** **She told Jessica she wanted to. And Jessica told**

28   **Rachel. And Rachel told Amy. Amy sits beside me in**

29   **choir.** *(Scales)* **La, la, la, la, la, la la!** *(As if talking to*

30   *Amy)* **Really? Tori wants to ask out Brett?** *(Sings.)* **La,**

31   **la, la, la, la, la, la!** *(As if talking to Amy)* **My Brett? My**

32   **best friend?** *(Sings.)* **La, la, la, la, la, la, la, la!** *(As if*

33   *talking to Amy)* **But he's dating Madison.** *(Sings.)* **La,**

34   **la, la, la, la, la, la!** *(As if talking to Amy)* **Tori thinks**

35   **Brett is hot?** *(Sings.)* **La, la, la, la, la, la, la, la.** *(As if*

1   *talking to Amy)* **But what about Madison?** *(Sings.)* **La,**
2   **la, la, la, la, la, la, la.** *(As if talking to Amy)* **Pass the**
3   **message along to Brett and see how he feels about it?**
4   *(Sings.)* **La, la, la, la, la, la, la, la.**
5 **BRETT: It's true?**
6 **NICK: According to Amy, Tori Welch has a thing for you.**
7 **BRETT: She thinks I'm hot?**
8 **NICK: According to Amy. And I think she's a pretty**
9   **reliable source. She's the one who told me Jade hated**
10   **my guts. And it was true.**
11 **BRETT: Really?**
12 **NICK: Really! I sent her a text message asking her to go to**
13   **the sports banquet with me. And you know what she**
14   **said? "No! And don't ever text me again!" I'd say that**
15   **text was pretty apparent that she hated my guts. Oh**
16   **well. Life goes on.**
17 **BRETT: Tori really has a thing for me?**
18 **NICK: Oh, and this was the other part I didn't tell you**
19   **about.**
20 **BRETT: What?**
21 **NICK: Then Amy turned to me and said, "Friday night**
22   **she's going to text Brett and ask him to her party. To**
23   **be her date."**
24 **BRETT: Tonight? Tonight, the same night I'm planning to**
25   **ask Madison to be my wife?**
26 **NICK: According to Amy. But don't worry about it. Just put**
27   **your phone on silent. And you can do what Jade did**
28   **to me. Text her and say, "No! And don't ever text me**
29   **again!"**
30 **BRETT: But Tori is ... is ... is ...**
31 **NICK: She's a babe.**
32 **BRETT: She is!**
33 **NICK: But you and Madison ... true love.**
34 **BRETT:** *(Looks at the ring box.)* **I thought so.**
35 **NICK: So why don't you practice on me. I'll be Madison.**

1   Ask me to marry you.

2   **BRETT: Uh ... I don't know.**

3   **NICK: Come on! You've got to have it all down so it comes**

4   **out right. What are you going to say?**

5   **BRETT: Uh ...**

6   **NICK: Madison ...**

7   **BRETT: Madison ...**

8   **NICK: Come on! Come on!**

9   **BRETT: Madison ...**

10   **NICK:** *(Drops to his knee as if he's BRETT.)* **Madison, will**

11   **you marry me?** *(Stands up as if he's Madison.)* **Will I?**

12   **Will I?** *(Drops to his knee.)* **Please say yes. You know I**

13   **love you.** *(Stands up.)* **Oh, Brett! Yes! Yes, I will!** *(Takes*

14   *the ring box from BRETT and falls to his knee.)* **For you,**

15   **Madison.** *(Stands up.)* **For me? Oh, Brett!** *(Opens the*

16   *box and stares inside it for a long time. NICK grabs the*

17   *magnifying glass and drops to his knee, holding out the*

18   *magnifying glass. He then jumps up, holding the*

19   *magnifying glass.)* **Thank you!** *(Holds the magnifying*

20   *glass up to look at the ring.)* **There it is! I see it! I love it!**

21   **Oh, Brett!** *(Pause, he looks at BRETT.)* **How was that?**

22   **BRETT: I think I changed my mind.**

23   **NICK: About asking Madison to accept your promise ring?**

24   **BRETT: Maybe I'm not ready. Maybe I am too young.**

25   **Maybe I need to wait.**

26   **NICK: Well, if you want my opinion ...**

27   **BRETT: You think I'm too young, don't you?**

28   **NICK: I think you're too young until you hit thirty-five or**

29   **forty!**

30   **BRETT:** *(Tosses the ring box aside.)* **I can't do it.**

31   **NICK: Maybe you and Madison need a break from each**

32   **other.**

33   **BRETT: Break up with Madison?**

34   **NICK: Freedom, man. Freedom.**

35   **BRETT: Five minutes ago I'm thinking about asking**

1   Madison to be my wife and now I'm considering
2   breaking up with her. What's wrong with me? Why
3   am I suddenly so confused?
4 NICK: Women will do that to you. But I'm not going to be
5   tied down to any girl. I need my space.
6 BRETT: Nick, you've never even had a girlfriend.
7 NICK: So? I still like my space. But if Tori Welch asked me
8   to be her date to her birthday party ...
9 BRETT: You'd say yes?
10 NICK: In a heartbeat! *(Sings.)* La, la, la, la, la, la, la!
11 BRETT: That's it. I've changed my mind. I don't want to be
12   promised or engaged or married. I want to be
13   available. I'm too young! I have life experiences to
14   experience.
15 NICK: Good choice, my friend.
16 BRETT: *(Picks up the ring box.)* I wonder if I can get a
17   refund back on this diamond ring?
18 NICK: Maybe. If not, just save it for the next girl you fall in
19   love with.
20 BRETT: Good idea.
21 NICK: *(Hands him the magnifying glass.)* And you better
22   hold onto this, too.
23 BRETT: I'll put them both in my underwear drawer. Just
24   in case.
25 NICK: And if Tori texts you tonight?
26 BRETT: If Tori texts me tonight, I'll say yes. Yes, yes, yes!
27 NICK: Dude, you are so not ready to be tied down.
28 BRETT: I know! And thanks for helping me figure that
29   out.
30 NICK: Any time.

19. Class President

CAST: (3F) NAIDA, RAYLEE, MRS. POPE
PROPS: Podium, note cards for Mrs. Pope
SETTING: School auditorium

1   *(At rise, NAIDA and RAYLEE are sitting in chairs on the*
2   *stage. MRS. POPE stands at the podium with a stack of*
3   *note cards, which she will use to ask the candidates*
4   *questions.)*
5   **MRS. POPE: Welcome, everyone. Welcome. Today we are**
6   **down to the final two candidates who are running for**
7   **sophomore class president. May I introduce to you,**
8   **Naida.** *(NAIDA stands and waves.)* **And Raylee.** *(RAYLEE*
9   *stands and waves.)* **In a moment I will be asking both**
10   **girls questions which have been submitted to us by the**
11   **sophomore class. But first I'm going to give each**
12   **candidate a moment to give a brief introduction.**
13   **Naida, you may go first.**
14   **NAIDA:** *(Steps up to the podium.)* **Thank you, Mrs. Pope. First**
15   **of all, I'm Naida and I'm running for sophomore class**
16   **president. I'm here today to tell you why I am the best**
17   **candidate for class president. First of all, there are too**
18   **many rules around this place. I think it's time the**
19   **school lightened up on the dress code and let us wear**
20   **what we want to wear. I also think we should have the**
21   **right to use the restroom whenever we need to. Why**
22   **should we be expected to hold it? And I also advocate**
23   **dances in the gym every Friday night. These are just a**
24   **few of the issues I plan to work on when you vote for**
25   **me as sophomore class president. Thank you.** *(Returns*
26   *to her chair.)*
27   **MRS. POPE: Raylee, you are next.**
28   **RAYLEE:** *(Goes to the podium.)* **Thank you, Mrs. Pope. I'm**
29   **Raylee and I would like your vote for sophomore class**

1   president. Why? Because it's time for a change. In the
2   past, voting for class president has always been a
3   popularity contest. Well, how about voting for
4   someone that is not popular? Someone who is like
5   you? Someone like me. I'm not in this to have my
6   picture in the yearbook or to get an attitude and
7   think that I'm all that ... that I'm better than you. I'm
8   in this for you. You deserve to have someone who
9   represents you. Yes, change is needed. And I, class,
10   am the change you need. Thank you. *(Returns to her*
11   *chair.)*
12 MRS. POPE: Thank you, girls. Now for the questions.
13   When I call your name, please stand and answer the
14   question. Naida. *(NAIDA stands.)* Question. How do
15   you feel about having ten minutes between classes?
16 NAIDA: Good question. I know many of my friends,
17   including myself, struggle with getting to their next
18   class in the time allotted. I believe the time between
19   classes should be extended. Students should not be
20   stressed by being forced to rush to their locker, the
21   restroom, and have a moment to chat with their
22   friends. This is why so many tardies are given each
23   semester. So if I am elected sophomore class
24   president, I will request ten minutes between each
25   class. Thank you. *(Sits.)*
26 MRS. POPE: Raylee, would you care to answer the
27   question? Do you have a different opinion?
28 RAYLEE: *(Stands.)* Yes, I do. I'm afraid ten minutes
29   between classes will not work. Those extra five
30   minutes will add up, forcing us to stay in school
31   longer each day. So instead of extending the school
32   day by thirty minutes or so, I say we continue to run
33   like mad to our next class. Hey, it's good exercise,
34   people. Thank you.
35 MRS. POPE: Thank you, Raylee. Please remain standing.

1   The next question is for you. How do you feel about
2   bringing soda and snack machines back into our
3   school?
4 RAYLEE: Unfortunately, I am not for this. I believe sales of
5   high calorie and zero nutrient snacks should be
6   prohibited. A student is not going to do well in class
7   when he or she is on a constant sugar high. Look
8   around. Many of us need to shed a few extra pounds.
9   Some of us need to shed a few more than that. But I
10   do believe the school should encourage healthy
11   eating habits. As an alternative, we could provide
12   healthy options. Such as fruit, vegetables, and yogurt
13   ... Thank you. *(Sits.)*
14 MRS. POPE: Naida, do you have a different view.
15 NAIDA: Yes, I do. *(Stands.)* Bring back those soda and
16   candy bar machines. Please! We are teenagers, for
17   goodness sake. Let us eat our junk food. We're going
18   to anyway! And the profits made off of these
19   machines would be enough to purchase needed items
20   for our schools. Computers, books for the library,
21   pizza parties! I am an individual and I have the right
22   to eat what I want. Don't take my sodas and candy
23   away. Thank you.
24 MRS. POPE: Naida, the next question is for you. *(NAIDA*
25   *continues to stand.)* Should students be allowed to
26   wear shorts to school?
27 NAIDA: Like, duh! And why shouldn't we be able to wear
28   shorts? Like our bare legs are a distraction? Besides,
29   many of the girls' skirts are so short already that they
30   might as well wear shorts. And that's not fair to boys.
31   Because girls can wear short skirts and stay cool, but
32   boys can't. Not that I'm advocating that guys wear
33   skirts, but I mean if they want to, they should be able
34   to. So yes, shorts should be acceptable. *(Sits.)*
35 MRS. POPE: Raylee?

1   RAYLEE: *(Stands.)* **Absolutely not. There is a time and**
2   **place for shorts and flip-flops and school is not it.**
3   **Let's have a little pride, people. I'm not suggesting**
4   **suits and ties or dresses, but I think students should**
5   **dress in a respectful and appropriate manner. Short**
6   **shorts do one thing. They keep getting shorter. So at**
7   **what point are you going to stop? The only way to**
8   **deal with this is to deny it. Thank you.** *(Sits down.)*
9   **NAIDA:** *(To RAYLEE)* **You are so going to lose this race.**
10   **RAYLEE: Why do you say that?**
11   **NAIDA: Because you sound like a teacher or a parent.**
12   **Students want freedom.**
13   **RAYLEE: Students need rules.**
14   **MRS. POPE: Naida, next question.** *(NAIDA stands.)* **What is**
15   **your opinion about the use of cell phones in school?**
16   **NAIDA: Everyone is doing it. Yeah, we're not supposed to,**
17   **but can the teachers really be that dumb? I mean,**
18   **when you turn around and half your class is hiding**
19   **behind their backpacks with their heads down ...**
20   **what do you think they're doing? Texting! So what's**
21   **the big deal? We're teenagers. We need to**
22   **communicate. We have dates to set up. Gossip to**
23   **share. People to ask out. And sadly, people to break**
24   **up with. So I believe cell phone use should be**
25   **allowed. Let us come out from behind our backpacks**
26   **and text in freedom. Thank you.** *(Sits down.)*
27   **MRS. POPE: Raylee?**
28   **RAYLEE:** *(Stands.)* **I believe cell phones should only be**
29   **allowed for emergencies. Our job is to come to school**
30   **to learn, not sneak around the teacher's back and**
31   **text when we should be paying attention. It's**
32   **disrespectful to the teachers who have worked so**
33   **hard to prepare class for that day. So, I'm sorry, I**
34   **cannot support the use of cell phones during class.**
35   *(Sits down.)*

1   NAIDA: *(To RAYLEE)* No one is going to vote for you.

2   RAYLEE: The only people who are going to vote for you are

3   the class clowns with no goals for the future. Except

4   to drink sodas and watch TV all day long. In their

5   pajama pants.

6   NAIDA: *(Stands.)* Mrs. Pope, may I bring up a topic that ties

7   into one of our previous discussions?

8   MRS. POPE: Yes, Naida. Go ahead.

9   NAIDA: Pajama pants.

10   MRS. POPE: Pajama pants?

11   NAIDA: Along with shorts, we should be allowed to wear

12   our pajama pants to school. And why not? They're

13   comfortable. They're not showing anything

14   inappropriate. And on those mornings you've

15   overslept, well, just crawl out of bed, grab your

16   backpack, and run out the door. No time for

17   breakfast? Heck, just grab a soda and candy bar at the

18   nearest vending machine. *(Sits.)*

19   MRS. POPE: Raylee? Your opinion.

20   RAYLEE: *(Stands.)* Sure, if we want to be a high school full

21   of slobs running around on sugar highs all day.

22   *(Looks around.)* Why are you clapping? Wearing your

23   pj's to school? I wouldn't clap about that! *(Sits.)*

24   MRS. POPE: All right, then. Let me find another question.

25   NAIDA: *(To RAYLEE)* Do you ever wonder why you're not

26   popular?

27   RAYLEE: I am popular among all my unpopular friends.

28   Which is ninety percent of the school. So you're the

29   one who's going to lose.

30   NAIDA: And who is it that's getting all the applause?

31   RAYLEE: The few popular students out there just happen

32   to clap very loudly.

33   NAIDA: That's so not true. The whole class was clapping.

34   You sound like another teacher. Rules, rules, rules.

35   Well, we want more freedom. More fun!

1 RAYLEE: And grow up to be what? An overweight slob
2   with no direction?
3 NAIDA: A happy kid makes a happy adult. That's my
4   motto. Give me the candy and let me come to school
5   in my pajamas. Life is good!
6 MRS. POPE: Next question. Raylee. *(RAYLEE stands.)* How
7   do you feel about PDA? PDA? What is PDA?
8 RAYLEE: I don't know, Mrs. Pope.
9 NAIDA: *(Jumps up.)* I know. *(To RAYLEE)* How can you not
10   know?
11 RAYLEE: I don't do a lot of texting. Unlike you, I study.
12 MRS. POPE: Naida, would you please tell us what PDA
13   stands for.
14 NAIDA: Public display of affection.
15 MRS. POPE: Oh! Such as holding hands or kissing?
16 NAIDA: Yes, ma'am.
17 MRS. POPE: All right, then. Raylee, how do you feel about
18   PDA?
19 RAYLEE: Disgusted. As for wearing shorts and pajamas to
20   class, there is a time and place for everything. Well,
21   almost everything. And making out in school is not
22   the time and place. Boys should keep their hands to
23   themselves and likewise the girls. We don't need to
24   see that lovey-dovey stuff at school. I know my
25   friends, my unpopular friends, which I mentioned is
26   ninety percent of the class, do not appreciate
27   watching you lovebirds pretend you're sitting at the
28   back of a movie theatre. Disgusting. So keep your
29   hands and your lips to yourself! *(Sits.)*
30 MRS. POPE: All right. Naida?
31 NAIDA: For crying out loud! We are teenagers, people. We
32   fall in love. We have the strong desire to hold our
33   boyfriend or girlfriend's hand. So what? And if we
34   have a little kiss between classes ... So what? We hug
35   our parents, sometimes our teachers, so let us hug

1   our boyfriends and girlfriends. And when did

2   holding hands become a crime? PDA? Yes! I support

3   PDA all the way. Thank you. *(Sits down.)*

4   RAYLEE: You are a parent's worst nightmare.

5   NAIDA: Whatever. I'm going to win. Even your unpopular

6   friends are going to vote for me.

7   RAYLEE: No way.

8   MRS. POPE: That's all the questions I have. Now I'm going

9   to give each one of you one last chance to highlight

10   your campaign. Raylee.

11   RAYLEE: *(Stands.)* Thank you, Mrs. Pope. As you have seen,

12   I firmly believe in rules and regulations. That's

13   because it's the only way to succeed and achieve the

14   goals and dreams that we long for. The future is ours

15   and together we will reach them! Thank you. *(Sits.)*

16   NAIDA: *(Stands. Raises hands.)* We are teenagers! We want

17   to have fun! Down with the strict rules and

18   regulations. Give us freedom and choices. Let me

19   wear my pajamas to school. Let us drink sodas and

20   eat candy. Let me kiss my boyfriend between classes.

21   And let me whip out my cell phone and text him

22   during class. Life should be fun. Especially when

23   you're a teen! Thank you! Thank you! Thank you!

24   *(Smiles.)* Wow! Everyone is clapping. Thank you! Go

25   teenagers!

20. Juliet Tryouts

CAST: (1M, 4F) EMILY, WILLOW, BLAIR, NICOLE, JARED
SETTING: Student center at school

1   EMILY: Willow, look at me.

2   WILLOW: What?

3   EMILY: Tell me. Do I look hideous?

4   WILLOW: What?

5   EMILY: Look at me. Look! Look!

6   WILLOW: What? What am I looking for?

7   EMILY: Don't you see the pimple on my face?

8   WILLOW: No.

9   EMILY: Do you swear you don't see it? Do you swear on your

10   life?

11   WILLOW: Yes and no.

12   EMILY: Yes and no?

13   WILLOW: Emily, I swear I can't see it, but I'm not swearing

14   on my life over your non-existent pimple.

15   EMILY: OK. OK. I'm overreacting.

16   WILLOW: Why? What's going on?

17   EMILY: I have drama tryouts today. And I must, must, must

18   get the lead.

19   WILLOW: What's the play?

20   EMILY: *Romeo and Juliet.* And of course I want to be Juliet.

21   And I swear, if I don't get the part, I will absolutely quit

22   school and move to the North Pole.

23   WILLOW: That's a bit dramatic, don't you think?

24   EMILY: Me, dramatic? I'm in drama, what do you expect?

25   WILLOW: How many girls are trying out?

26   EMILY: Fourteen. Can you believe that? Fourteen girls

27   trying out for the role of Juliet. Willow, I want that part!

28   I must have that part. If I don't ... oh, if I don't ...

29   WILLOW: You're going to quit school.

30   EMILY: And move to the South Pole.

1 WILLOW: I thought you said you were moving to the North
2   Pole.
3 EMILY: North, south, whatever.
4 BLAIR: *(Enters.)* Emily, are we ready for auditions?
5 EMILY: Am I ready for auditions? Of course I'm ready.
6 WILLOW: Hi, Blair. Are you trying out for Juliet as well?
7 BLAIR: Of course. I was made to play the role of Juliet.
8 EMILY: So was I.
9 BLAIR: And just to make sure I have perfected this role,
10   my mother has been sending me to a drama coach at
11   the university.
12 EMILY: What? You've been seeing a drama coach?
13 BLAIR: Yes. Mother insisted. The coach says I'm perfect
14   for the part. *(Dramatically)* "Romeo, Romeo!
15   Wherefore art thou Romeo?"
16 EMILY: The part was made for me! *(Dramatically)* "Romeo,
17   Romeo! Wherefore art thou Romeo?"
18 BLAIR: *(Steps forward. Dramatically)* "Deny thy father and
19   refuse thy name!"
20 EMILY: *(Steps in front of BLAIR. Dramatically)* "Or if thou
21   wilt not, be but sworn my love!"
22 BLAIR: *(Steps in front of EMILY. Dramatically)* "And I'll no
23   longer be a Capulet!"
24 WILLOW: *(Claps.)* You are both good.
25 EMILY: Willow, who do you think was the best?
26 WILLOW: You were both good.
27 NICOLE: *(Enters.)* Only a couple more hours till I tryout for
28   Juliet.
29 WILLOW: You too, Nicole?
30 NICOLE: *(Dramatically)* "Romeo, Romeo! Wherefore art
31   thou Romeo?"
32 BLAIR: *(Steps in front of NICOLE.)* "Deny thy father and
33   refuse thy name!"
34 EMILY: *(Steps in front of BLAIR.)* "Or if thou wilt not, be but
35   sworn my love!"

1   **NICOLE:** *(Steps in front of EMILY.)* **"And I'll no longer be a**
2   **Capulet!"**
3   **WILLOW: Wow. You are all good. And there are fourteen**
4   **girls trying out for one part ... that's tough.**
5   **NICOLE: Yes. Very.**
6   **BLAIR: And only three boys are auditioning for Romeo.**
7   **EMILY: Why is it always like that?**
8   **WILLOW: Wow. The girls have a lot of competition. And**
9   **like I said, you are all good.**
10 **EMILY:** *(Throwing her arms out)* **But only one will be**
11   **awarded the role of Juliet.**
12 **NICOLE: The girl with the most talent.**
13 **BLAIR: Here I am! Juliet.**
14 **EMILY: I will be Juliet.**
15 **NICOLE: I've got this role down. There's no stopping me.**
16   *(Steps forward.)* **"Good night, good night! Parting is**
17   **such sweet sorrow."**
18 **BLAIR and EMILY:** *(Both step forward and fight to stand in the*
19   *front)* **"That I shall say good night till it be morrow!"**
20 **NICOLE: There can only be one Juliet. And that will be me.**
21 **BLAIR:** *(Steps in front of NICOLE.)* **No, me.**
22 **EMILY:** *(Steps in front of BLAIR.)* **Juliet? That is me!**
23   **"What's in a name? That which we call a rose, By any**
24   **other name would smell as sweet."**
25 **WILLOW: Mrs. Tatum sure is going to have a hard**
26   **decision.**
27 **NICOLE: "Romeo, Romeo ... "**
28 **BLAIR: "Wherefore art thou Romeo?"**
29 **EMILY: That's *my* Romeo!**
30 **NICOLE: No! It's *my* Romeo.**
31 **BLAIR: *My* Romeo.**
32 **JARED:** *(Enters. He is sloppily dressed.)* **Romeo has arrived.**
33 **WILLOW: Hi Jared. Are you trying out for Romeo?**
34 **JARED: Yes I am. And I will be the *only* one trying out for**
35   **the part.**

1   EMILY: What?

2   BLAIR: But we heard there were three boys trying out for

3   the part of Romeo.

4   JARED: Well, Casey has the flu and David backed out. So

5   that would leave me. *(Badly, with a cracked voice)* "But

6   soft! What light through yonder window breaks? It is

7   the East and Juliet is the sun! Arise fair sun and kill

8   the envious moon." I memorized that on the way to

9   school this morning. Good, huh?

10   NICOLE: This is a tragedy.

11   EMILY: Jared, you're the only one trying out for Romeo?

12   JARED: Tis I.

13   WILLOW: Have you been in any other plays?

14   JARED: This play shall be my first. So, which one of you

15   beautiful ladies shall be my Juliet? *(Silence)*

16   BLAIR: Casey's sick?

17   NICOLE: And David changed his mind?

18   EMILY: And you're the only one trying out? A freshman

19   who's never spent a day in theatre? Who doesn't know

20   stage right from stage left?

21   JARED: I can figure out right stage from left stage. *(Thinks*

22   *about this for a moment. Points.)* Right ... left. Or is that

23   left ... right?

24   BLAIR: Jared, when did you decide to tryout?

25   JARED: Well, I just woke up this morning and decided to

26   go for it. I went by Mrs. Tatum's class first and told

27   her I wanted to tryout for the role of Romeo.

28   BLAIR: Just like that? But you've had no training. Or

29   experience.

30   JARED: Just like that! And Mrs. Tatum said, "Wonderful!"

31   Because I was now the only guy trying out for a role

32   of a lifetime. So do you know what that means?

33   *(Silence)* I'm Romeo! "Romeo, Romeo, where for art

34   thou Romeo?"

35   NICOLE: That's not your line, Jared.

1　JARED: "Good night, good night! Parting is such sweet
2　　　　sorrow that I shall say good night till it be tomorrow."
3　　　　I memorized that line too. I'm quick at memorizing
4　　　　aren't I?
5　EMILY: Jared, that's not your line, either. It's Juliet's.
6　JARED: Oh well. At least I'm good at memorizing.
7　WILLOW: Well, isn't this interesting. I guess Mrs. Tatum
8　　　　will probably look at who has the most chemistry
9　　　　with Jared. So it will be more believable.
10　JARED: Come to me, girls. Let's see who's got the most
11　　　　chemistry with me. *(The girls step back)* "Out,
12　　　　damned spot! out, I say! One; two: why, then, 'tis time
13　　　　to do 't. Hell is murky! Fie, my lord, fie!"
14　BLAIR: Jared! That isn't from *Romeo and Juliet.*
15　WILLOW: I know that one. It's from *Macbeth.* But you just
16　　　　said the part of Lady Macbeth.
17　JARED: Oops. Like I said, I memorize stuff easy. I can
18　　　　memorize my parts, your parts. Hey, if you forget
19　　　　your line during the play, I can whisper it to you.
20　　　　Because I'll have everyone's parts memorized! So
21　　　　which one of you girls wants to check out your
22　　　　chemistry with me? *(The GIRLS step back.)* Don't be
23　　　　shy. "Romeo, Romeo, where for art thou Romeo?"
24　NICOLE: That's not your line, Jared.
25　EMILY: I'm depressed.
26　BLAIR: Me too.
27　NICOLE: Me three.
28　WILLOW: I'm even depressed and I wasn't even trying out
29　　　　for Juliet.
30　JARED: Just call me Romeo. And which of you girls wants
31　　　　to be my Juliet? Come to me, Juliet. *(The GIRLS step*
32　　　　*back.)* "Juliet, my love! Where are you? If I might steal
33　　　　but a kiss! Oh, to be in your arms." Yeah, I made that
34　　　　part up, but it sounded good, didn't it? "Juliet! Come
35　　　　to me, my love!" *(EMILY, BLAIR, and NICOLE turn and*
36　　　　*exit.)*

1   **WILLOW: Looks like you're on your own, Jared.** *(She exits.)*
2   **JARED:** *(Holding out his arms)* **Juliet! Come back to me, my**
3   **love.** *(Pause)* **"Good night, good night! Parting is such**
4   **sweet sorrow that I shall say good night till it be**
5   **morrow."**

21. Breaking Up Is Hard to Do

CAST: (3M, 2F) MIA, PAIGE, ZACH, HUNTER, CODY
PROPS: Notebook paper, cell phone, cup of coffee
SETTING: Coffee house

1   (At rise, PAIGE is reading a letter. MIA enters.)

2   **MIA: Mia has arrived!**

3   **PAIGE:** (Crumples up paper.) **Mia, my life is over.**

4   **MIA: What happened, Paige? Bad grade? Hey, it happens to**
5   **the best of us. We'll figure out a way to break the bad**
6   **news to your mom. Two great minds that think alike. I**
7   **know! "Mom, I guess I'm dumb. I tried so hard, but I**
8   **just didn't understand. Mom, can you still love a dumb**
9   **daughter? No, you probably can't. Just give me away,**
10   **Mom. Adopt me out or something. You don't want a**
11   **dumb daughter." Then she'll feel sorry for you and the**
12   **topic will switch to how much she loves you, not about**
13   **how you totally flunked an assignment. So ... feel**
14   **better?**

15   **PAIGE: Mia, it's not that. My grades are fine.**

16   **MIA: Then what is it?**

17   **PAIGE:** (Holding out the crumpled piece of paper) **This.**

18   **MIA: And that is?**

19   **PAIGE: A note from Chris.**

20   **MIA: A note? Who writes notes? Why didn't he just text you?**

21   **PAIGE: I guess because a text felt too impersonal.**

22   **MIA: What did Chris say?**

23   **PAIGE:** (About to cry) **What did he say? You want to hear**
24   **what he said?** (Opens letter and straightens it out to
25   read.)

26   **MIA: Yes. Tell me what he said.**

27   **PAIGE: Listen to this! "Paige, first let me tell you how much**
28   **you mean to me ... "**

29   **MIA: Uh-oh. It's a break-up letter, isn't it?**

1   PAIGE: "Your friendship, support, long talks on the
2   phone, the laughing, the snow cones we shared ... "
3   Blue coconut was our favorite.
4   MIA: Why is he doing this? After almost two years!
5   PAIGE: *(Reading)* "But Paige, I must be honest with you.
6   I've been feeling the need to move on."
7   MIA: You think it's another girl?
8   PAIGE: Of course it's another girl! *(Reading)* "I need to soar
9   into the universe toward uncharted territory."
10 MIA: How stupid!
11 PAIGE: *(Reading)* "Discover new opportunities and
12   dreams that lie ahead."
13 MIA: Couldn't Chris have kept it simple? "Hey, it's over. I'm
14   breaking up. See ya."
15 PAIGE: *(Reading)* "New adventures! Unforeseen lands!"
16 MIA: Unforeseen girls is what I'm thinking.
17 PAIGE: *(Reading)* "But with all that said, Paige. I'll always
18   love you. Forever and ever, Chris."
19 MIA: Forever and ever?
20 PAIGE: *(Crumples paper and throws it.)* I hate him!
21 MIA: Do you want me to call him and find out what's really
22   going on?
23 PAIGE: No. I'm never speaking to him again.
24 MIA: OK, OK. I understand.
25 PAIGE: And I'll never trust another boy again. I hate boys!
26 MIA: Well, you need some time to grieve. The best advice I
27   can offer to you is don't call him, don't text him, and
28   don't email him. At all. And if you see him, act as if
29   you are as happy as ever. As if you don't even care that
30   he broke up with you.
31 PAIGE: *(Nodding)* I'll try.
32 MIA: No, you've got to, Paige. You can't let Chris think you
33   are even bothered by this break up. Believe me, that's
34   the perfect revenge. Because stalking, begging, and
35   crying don't work. It only makes you look like a

1   desperate fool.
2 PAIGE: Mia, I know you're right. I just wish I knew why.
3   After two years ...
4 MIA: I think he was pretty clear on his explanation. He
5   wants to soar into uncharted territory. Paige, he
6   wants to date other girls. Maybe the two of you have
7   been in a rut. Maybe he needs to stretch his wings
8   and see what's out there. He'll probably come
9   running back to you within a day. But that doesn't
10   matter. You need to do the same thing. Stretch your
11   wings. See what's out there.
12 PAIGE: I don't like anything that's out there.
13 MIA: Oh, you say that right now, but give yourself a
14   chance. Look over there at those two boys. I say cute,
15   cute, cute! Wouldn't you?
16 PAIGE: I don't know.
17 MIA: Let's walk over there and accidentally stop by and
18   say hello.
19 PAIGE: I don't want to, Mia.
20 MIA: Well, well, well ... look who just entered the coffee
21   shop with a new girlfriend.
22 PAIGE: *(Looks.)* Chris? What's he doing with her?
23 MIA: Ready to make some new friends?
24 PAIGE: *(Jumps up.)* Yes I am! *(PAIGE and MIA walk over to*
25   *the next table where ZACH and HUNTER are sitting.*
26   *PAIGE sits between the two boys.)* New around here?
27 MIA: We were wondering if you two boys went to our
28   school? You don't look familiar.
29 ZACH: We go to Carson Junior College. Is that where you
30   go too?
31 MIA: *(Excited)* College boys!
32 PAIGE: *(Looking toward Chris, then draping her arm*
33   *around HUNTER.)* So, tell me, what's your name?
34 HUNTER: *(Offers his hand.)* Hunter.
35 PAIGE: *(Removes her arm from his shoulder and takes his*

1	*hand.)* **Nice to meet you.** *(Doesn't let his hand go, even*
2	*though he tries.)* **Strong hands. Do you play football?**
3	**HUNTER: Baseball.**
4	**PAIGE:** *(Still holding his hand, often looking toward Chris to*
5	*see if he's watching)* **I love baseball.**
6	**HUNTER: That's good.** *(Trying to remove his hand from her*
7	*grip)*
8	**PAIGE: Yes, you have strong hands.**
9	**HUNTER: Yeah ... uh, thanks.**
10	**PAIGE: I love strong hands.**
11	**HUNTER: I can see that. You're pretty strong yourself.**
12	*(Really struggling to get his hand away from her)*
13	**PAIGE: Do you want to pretend my hand is a baseball and**
14	**show me how you grip the ball?**
15	**HUNTER: No, not really.**
16	**PAIGE: It'd be fun! Or I can pretend your hand is a**
17	**baseball and show you how I'd grip it.**
18	**HUNTER: You know what, that's OK. Let's not.**
19	**PAIGE:** *(Looking toward Chris)* **But it's fun.**
20	**HUNTER:** *(Struggles to finally get his hand free.)* **Thank you!**
21	*(Shakes out his hand.)* **Wow.**
22	**ZACH: Where do you girls go to school?**
23	**MIA: Oh, just down the street.**
24	**ZACH: High school?**
25	**MIA: Seniors.**
26	**PAIGE: Yeah, we're seniors.**
27	**ZACH: Right. Well, we've gotta take off, girls. Nice to meet**
28	**you.**
29	**HUNTER: See you around.** *(They exit.)*
30	**PAIGE: So much for making Chris jealous. I don't even**
31	**think he looked this way.**
32	**MIA: Don't worry about him.**
33	**PAIGE: After two years I shouldn't worry about him?**
34	**Maybe I should call him while he's with his new**
35	**girlfriend.** *(Takes out phone.)* **That's what I'll do!**

1   MIA: *(Takes her phone.)* **Oh, no you don't! And stop looking**
2   **at him. Look at me. Paige, look at me!**
3   **PAIGE: I'm looking at you.** *(Looks at Chris.)*
4   **MIA: Look at me!**
5   **PAIGE: OK! I'm looking at you.** *(Staring at MIA)* **Do you see**
6   **the tear that's about to fall down my cheek?**
7   **MIA: Yes, but don't let it fall. Do not let it slip out of your**
8   **eye. Fight it back!**
9   **PAIGE:** *(Blinking fast)* **You know what I want to do?**
10   **MIA: Look at me.**
11   **PAIGE: I'm looking at you!**
12   **MIA: You glanced at him.**
13   **PAIGE: I'm sorry. What I want to do is run over there and**
14   **punch him.**
15   **MIA: But we aren't going to do that because we don't care**
16   **who he's with. We are over Chris. Remember?**
17   **PAIGE:** *(Looks at Chris.)* **I forgot ...**
18   **MIA: Paige, look at me.**
19   **PAIGE:** *(Looks at MIA, with gritted teeth.)* **I'm looking at**
20   **you!**
21   **MIA: There's another tear. Blink it away right now.**
22   **PAIGE:** *(Blinking fast)* **I'm trying. So I can't call him?**
23   **MIA: No!**
24   **PAIGE: I can't run over there and punch him?**
25   **MIA: No!**
26   **PAIGE: Can I run over and throw my arms around him**
27   **and beg him to take me back?**
28   **MIA:** *(Grabs her hands.)* **No, you cannot.**
29   **PAIGE: Then what am I supposed to do besides fight back**
30   **these tears and stare at you?**
31   **CODY:** *(Enters.)* **Hey, Mia. Hey, Paige.**
32   **MIA: Hi Cody.**
33   **PAIGE: Hi.**
34   **CODY:** *(To PAIGE)* **So, I hear you and Chris broke up.**
35   **MIA: It was a mutual decision. Time to move on.**

1   CODY: I'm glad.

2   PAIGE: You are?

3   CODY: *(Nods.)* I'm glad you want to move on. I've been

4   waiting for my chance.

5   PAIGE: Your chance?

6   CODY: To ask you out.

7   PAIGE: You have?

8   CODY: I have. So ...

9   PAIGE: So ... ?

10 MIA: She'd love to!

11 CODY: You would?

12 PAIGE: *(Looks at MIA.)* What would I love to do?

13 MIA: She'd love to go out with you.

14 CODY: Perfect. Let's start now. Let me buy you a cup of

15   coffee.

16 MIA: She'd love it.

17 CODY: You like caramel in your coffee, right?

18 PAIGE: How did you know?

19 CODY: I pay attention. Mia, can I get you something?

20 MIA: No, I'm fine. Thank you.

21 CODY: I'll be right back.

22 MIA: Wow! That was fast!

23 PAIGE: I know! And you know what? All of a sudden I'm

24   feeling kind of excited and happy that Chris and I

25   broke up. Now I can soar into the universe toward

26   uncharted territory.

27 MIA: And Cody is a cute uncharted territory.

28 PAIGE: I know! I never even thought about liking someone

29   else before, but now ... And did you hear what he said?

30   Cody knew I liked caramel in my coffee because he

31   pays attention.

32 MIA: I guess he's had a crush on you for a long time. Oh,

33   and by the way, guess who's been looking over here at

34   you ever since Cody came over here?

35 PAIGE: Chris?

1 MIA: That's right.
2 PAIGE: *(Sits up straight.)* **Well, good. I could care less if he's**
3   **jealous or happy or sad. And look into my eyes, Mia.**
4   **No more tears!**
5 MIA: Good! And I say good riddance.
6 PAIGE: And I say now I'm going to discover new
7   opportunities and dreams that lie ahead.
8 MIA: Thanks to Chris.
9 PAIGE: Yes. Thanks to Chris.

22. Excuses

CAST: (2M) MR. CRUMPLEY, CARTER
PROPS: Paper
SETTING: Principal's office

1   *(At rise, CARTER enters the principal's office.)*
2   **MR. CRUMPLEY: Carter, sit down.**
3   **CARTER: Can I stand?**
4   **MR. CRUMPLEY: Sit down.**
5   **CARTER:** *(Sits.)* **Yes sir.**
6   **MR. CRUMPLEY:** *(Looking at a sheet of paper)* **Carter, you've**
7   **had nine tardies in one week.**
8   **CARTER: Yes sir.**
9   **MR. CRUMPLEY: Nine.**
10   **CARTER: Yes sir.**
11   **MR. CRUMPLEY: Do you have an excuse?**
12   **CARTER: Yes sir. I have nine excuses actually.**
13   **MR. CRUMPLEY: Nine?**
14   **CARTER: For the nine tardies. Nine different reasons. Good**
15   **reasons, I might add.**
16   **MR. CRUMPLEY: I'll be the judge of that.**
17   **CARTER: Yes sir.**
18   **MR. CRUMPLEY: Carter, let me tell you that I've heard every**
19   **excuse in the book and none have been sufficient**
20   **enough for a dismissal. Not one.**
21   **CARTER: But my excuses are valid, Mr. Crumpley. Uh ... sir.**
22   **MR. CRUMPLEY:** *(Looking at the sheet of paper again, shaking*
23   *his head)* **Nine tardies in one week. How does one do**
24   **that?**
25   **CARTER: Mr. Crumpley, have you ever had one of those**
26   **weeks?**
27   **MR. CRUMPLEY: One of those weeks?**
28   **CARTER: Yes. One of those weeks where everything goes**
29   **wrong.**

1   MR. CRUMPLEY: It's a daily thing for me, Carter.

2   CARTER: Well, that's what happened to me. It's like that

3   old saying, "When it rains, it pours." Well, kinda ...

4   MR. CRUMPLEY: Carter, what are you talking about?

5   CARTER: I'm trying to tell you that this week has just

6   been one of those weeks.

7   MR. CRUMPLEY: I can relate to that.

8   CARTER: *(Stands.)* Then you understand?

9   MR. CRUMPLEY: Sit down.

10 CARTER: *(Sits.)* What I'm saying, Mr. Crumpley ... sir ... is

11   that this isn't one of those weeks I'd like to repeat.

12   And thank goodness it's Friday.

13 MR. CRUMPLEY: Saturday detention is tomorrow so I

14   wouldn't get so excited about it being Friday if I were

15   you.

16 CARTER: Detention?

17 MR. CRUMPLEY: *(Shaking the paper)* Nine tardies, Carter.

18 CARTER: I know, I know. But you've got to hear me out,

19   Mr. Crumpley. Sir.

20 MR. CRUMPLEY: Make it snappy, Carter. There are other

21   students I need to see. But none with as many tardies

22   as you.

23 CARTER: OK, here's what happened. So Monday I was on

24   my way to class when my cell phone rings. Well,

25   vibrated, actually.

26 MR. CRUMPLEY: Emergency?

27 CARTER: No sir.

28 MR. CRUMPLEY: And do you not know the school's policy

29   about cell phone use? Only for emergencies.

30 CARTER: I know, Mr. Crumpley. So when my phone

31   started vibrating in my pocket, that's what I thought.

32   Emergency! Maybe someone got into a car accident.

33   Maybe someone died. Maybe something terrible has

34   happened.

35 MR. CRUMPLEY: And who was it that called you?

1 CARTER: Believe it or not, Mr. Crumpley, it was a phone
2   solicitor.
3 MR. CRUMPLEY: And you answered that call?
4 CARTER: It came up unknown. How was I supposed to
5   know it was a solicitor? So long story short, the
6   conversation went a little long and that's what caused
7   me to be late to class.
8 MR. CRUMPLEY: You mean to tell me you were talking to
9   a solicitor?
10 CARTER: Yes! Can you believe that? I mean, can you
11   believe they'd have the nerve to call a student during
12   school?
13 MR. CRUMPLEY: Then why didn't you hang up?
14 CARTER: I thought about doing that.
15 MR. CRUMPLEY: But what? You got suckered into one of
16   those high-pressured sales and offered them your
17   credit card number when you should have been
18   sitting in math class?
19 CARTER: No, no, it wasn't like that. I was telling off the
20   phone solicitor. I was telling her that she just called a
21   minor between classes and I was highly offended.
22   "This is my personal cell phone! How dare you call
23   me during school! Do you not care about my
24   education? No, I don't want your stupid magazine!"
25   Well, by the time we hung up, that lady was in tears. I
26   put her in her place. So that's why I was late to math
27   class.
28 MR. CRUMPLEY: Again, let me remind you that we have a
29   strict policy regarding cell phone use during school
30   hours.
31 CARTER: I know, and that's what I told the solicitor. I said,
32   "Put me on your do not call list. And if you call me
33   again, I'm going to tell my principal, Mr. Crumpley,
34   what you did and you will be sor-ry."
35 MR. CRUMPLEY: OK, there's one excuse.

1   CARTER: OK. Excuse number two. So I was headed to
2   class when Cassie lost her hairpiece or extension or
3   whatever it is you call it in the hallway. You know that
4   long fake ponytail? It just fell right off in front of me.
5   So, I picked it up and I was like, "Hey, Cassie, you lost
6   your ponytail. See. I have it. It fell on the ground in
7   front of me. Cassie? Hey, Cassie. Here's your hair."
8   MR. CRUMPLEY: And what does a fake ponytail have to do
9   with you being late to class?
10 CARTER: Because, Cassie turned around and unleashed
11   on me. Right there in the middle of the crowded
12   hallway. She started screaming, "You jerk! You didn't
13   have to tell the whole world." I was like, "I was just
14   trying to help, Cassie. And I can help you stick it back
15   on your head if you want me to." So that's what I
16   started doing. Trying to stick that ponytail wig thingy
17   back on top of her head. Well, she just started
18   screaming at me again. "Stop it! Stop it!" And then ...
19   then she started hitting me. She was like this!
20   *(Swings his arms like a girl.)* "Ouch! Quit!" Then she
21   snatched the ponytail out of my hand just as the bell
22   was ringing and ran into class. And there I stood in
23   the empty hallway. And I was just trying to be a
24   friend. So much for that.
25 MR. CRUMPLEY: That's two excuses. You still have seven
26   more to account for.
27 CARTER: OK. Here's the next one. I was on my way to class
28   when Marci, my girlfriend, jumped in front of me,
29   hands on hips, and said, "We have to talk!" Mr.
30   Crumpley, have you ever dealt with a woman who is
31   demanding to talk right then and right there?
32 MR. CRUMPLEY: Oh, yes.
33 CARTER: So I'm like, "What? I'm going to be late for class.
34   And if I get a third tardy that means detention. So
35   what do you want, Marci? And can you make it fast,

1   because I've got to go." Wrong thing to say. Believe
2   me. Because then she just went on and on and on and
3   on. "You hang out with your friends more than me. I
4   text you a hundred times more than you text me. You
5   hardly ever say you love me anymore. And did you
6   forget that today was my birthday?" I was about to tell
7   her the day was not over, but she didn't give me a
8   chance. "I'm sick of this one-sided relationship,
9   Carter. We are over." She stomps off to class and I'm
10   left standing there with my mouth wide open. Bell
11   rings. Late again. Number three!

12 MR. CRUMPLEY: And number four?

13 CARTER: So I'm headed to chemistry and Audrey says,
14   *(Sweet tone)* "Hey, can we talk?" I'm looking at my
15   watch, thinking I have thirty spare seconds. And I'm
16   like, "Sure, Audrey." Because she's one hot babe, Mr.
17   Crumpley. You know? I mean, sir. So anyway, she's
18   like, "I'm sorry you and Marci broke up." I'm like,
19   well, those things happen. Wondering why is Audrey
20   talking to me? Me? Does she want something?
21   Homework help? And then she said, "I think we
22   should hook up." Can you believe that, Mr. Crumpley?
23   Audrey wanted to hook up with me. Me!

24 MR. CRUMPLEY: No, I can't believe that.

25 CARTER: And I'm like, "Sure." All casually of course as if I
26   can take her or I can leave her, but inside I'm
27   screaming, "Audrey just asked me out! Yippee! I'm on
28   top of the world!" So she says, "Great. I'll text ya
29   during class."

30 MR. CRUMPLEY: *(Growls.)* Texting during class?

31 CARTER: Audrey said it, not me. So anyway, all of a sudden
32   I go from being dumped to going out with Audrey.
33   Can you believe that? So I'm standing in the hallway
34   doing a little happy dance and guess what happens?

35 MR. CRUMPLEY: The bell rings.

1 CARTER: That's right! Late again. Fourth time. I'm
2   thinking, I'm in big trouble now.
3 MR. CRUMPLEY: I'd agree. Fifth excuse?
4 CARTER: So, I'm walking to class ... I do that a lot don't I?
5 MR. CRUMPLEY: Yes, you walk to class a lot. You just don't
6   make it there on time.
7 CARTER: So I'm walking to class and Marci pulls on my
8   arm. I look at her and tears are streaming down her
9   face. "Carter, can we please talk?" What am I
10   supposed to do, Mr. Crumpley? My ex-girlfriend is
11   crying her eyes out?
12 MR. CRUMPLEY: Let me guess. You stopped to talk to her.
13 CARTER: Yes. I have to. I'm like, "What's wrong, Marci?
14   Are you all right?" Well, no she wasn't. She loved me
15   and she wanted me back. She heard through the text
16   grapevine that I was going out with Audrey now.
17 MR. CRUMPEY: Text grapevine?
18 CARTER: Oh, it's just a saying. So you have to understand
19   that Marci and I have been together for eight
20   months. And in all honesty, my heart is still with her.
21   So I tell her we can kiss and make up ... not literally
22   kiss because I know the school policy about kissing
23   on campus. So we agree to get back together. I wipe
24   away her tears and she runs off to class.
25 MR. CRUMPLEY: Why didn't you run off to class?
26 CARTER: Too far. The gym was on the other side of the
27   building. I knew I'd never make it. And then of
28   course you know what happened.
29 MR. CRUMPLEY: The bell rings.
30 CARTER: Correct. Late again. Fifth tardy. I'm in deep
31   trouble now.
32 MR. CRUMPLEY: Next?
33 CARTER: Well, this is a valid excuse.
34 MR. CRUMPLEY: I'll be the judge of that.
35 CARTER: Mr. Crumpley, I had to break up with Audrey

1   now that Marci and I were back together. I didn't
2   want to do it by text messaging. *(Thinks.)* Besides, I
3   don't text during class.
4 MR. CRUMPLEY: Right.
5 CARTER: So I found Audrey and explained to her that it
6   was over. And you know what she said?
7 MR. CRUMPLEY: *(Dryly)* I'm dying to know.
8 CARTER: She was like, "OK, fine." Gee, you'd think she
9   could've cried or something.
10 MR. CRUMPLEY: And why didn't you hurry off to class
11   after you dumped Audrey?
12 CARTER: Mr. Crumpley, it took longer than I expected.
13 MR. CRUMPLEY: It took longer than you expected to hear,
14   "OK, fine"?
15 CARTER: No, but it took longer than I expected to find
16   Audrey in the hallway. I didn't know her schedule. So
17   by the time I broke up with her and she said "OK,
18   fine," guess what happened?
19 MR. CRUMPLEY: The bell rang.
20 CARTER: Unfortunately yes. Major trouble now. Sixth
21   tardy.
22 MR. CRUMPLEY: Next.
23 CARTER: I know you'll excuse the next one. I had to go, if
24   you know what I mean.
25 MR. CRUMPLEY: To the bathroom?
26 CARTER: Yes! And I'm sorry, but it took longer than I
27   expected. There I was ... well, finishing up ... and the
28   bell rang. That could not have been helped, Mr.
29   Crumpley.
30 MR. CRUMPLEY: Next.
31 CARTER: The eighth tardy is not my fault, either.
32 MR. CRUMPLEY: I'm sure. Girlfriend problems again?
33 CARTER: No. Teacher problems. Mrs. Miller stopped me
34   in the hallway to gripe me out for being late to her
35   class. I was thinking, "Mrs. Miller, you're going to

1   make me late for class. Let it go already." But no. She

2   chewed me out one side and the other. Then the bell

3   rang and she said, "Now get to class!" So I was late

4   again. And it wasn't even my fault.

5 MR. CRUMPLEY: Eight excuses so far. And your last?

6 CARTER: My locker.

7 MR. CRUMPLEY: Your locker?

8 CARTER: Stuck!

9 MR. CRUMPLEY: Stuck?

10 CARTER: Yes sir. And I had to get it open because the

11   paper I needed to turn in to history class was inside

12   that locker. I'm telling you, I was having a major

13   battle with that stupid thing. I beat on it, kicked it,

14   begged it to open ... but nothing I did worked. And

15   then Phillip came along and saw what I was doing

16   and he gave it a Fonzie hit and it opened! Can you

17   believe that? So I opened my locker, grabbed my

18   paper, and guess what happened.

19 MR. CRUMPLEY: The bell rang?

20 CARTER: Exactly! I was thinking, "Great! I'm dead now."

21   *(Stands.)* But I think all my excuses are excusable,

22   don't you, Mr. Crumpley? Sir?

23 MR. CRUMPLEY: Sit! *(CARTER sits.)* Actually, yes.

24 CARTER: Yes?

25 MR. CRUMPLEY: Your excuses were the most interesting

26   and believable I have ever heard. And, for the first

27   time in my years of being a principal, I'm going to

28   excuse your tardies.

29 CARTER: You are?

30 MR. CRUMPLEY: *(Signs the paper.)* Yes I am.

31 CARTER: Thank you Mr. Crumpley!

32 MR. CRUMPLEY: And Carter ...

33 CARTER: Yes sir?

34 MR. CRUMPLEY: From now on ... get to class on time.

35 CARTER: Yes sir!

23. What Are Friends For?

CAST: (1M, 2F) EMMA, ISABEL, BLAKE
SETTING: School hallway

1   **EMMA:** *(To ISABEL)* **Pretend I'm Blake.**

2   **ISABEL: Why?**

3   **EMMA: Just do it. I'm Blake ...**

4   **ISABEL: Can I be me? Or do you want me to be Heather,**

5   **Blake's girlfriend? On second thought, that doesn't feel**

6   **right. You be Blake if you want to, but I'm being me.**

7   **EMMA: OK, I'm Blake. So, Isabel, tell me how you feel.**

8   **ISABEL: About what?**

9   **EMMA: About me.**

10   **ISABEL: How do I feel about you? Well, Emma, you're my**

11   **best friend. Sometimes you instigate things and get me**

12   **into trouble ... or grounded ... but I love you, BFF.**

13   **EMMA: Not how do you feel about me, but how do you feel**

14   **about Blake. *(Lowers voice.)* Tell me how you feel about**

15   **me.**

16   **ISABEL: You're strange, Emma. Very strange.**

17   **EMMA: I'm Blake! OK? *(Lowers voice.)* Tell me how you feel**

18   **about me.**

19   **ISABEL: Why?**

20   **EMMA: Just do it, Isabel! *(Lowers voice.)* How do you feel**

21   **about me?**

22   **ISABEL: Emma!**

23   **EMMA: I'm Blake!**

24   **ISABEL: But Blake's not going to ask me how I feel about**

25   **him. He has a girlfriend. Remember? Hello.**

26   **EMMA: They are on rocky territory. Fighting in Spanish**

27   **class this morning.**

28   **ISABEL: About what?**

29   **EMMA: Him ignoring her between second and third period.**

30   **ISABEL: They'll work it out.**

1　EMMA: I don't know. Heather turned around and told
2　　　Mia, who sits next to me, that she's finished with
3　　　Blake. She was moving on. Said it like this ... *(Imitates*
4　　　*Heather, speaking quietly, angry)* "I have had it with
5　　　you-know-who. He's hot. He's cold. Before school he
6　　　loves me, then after third period he can't find two
7　　　words to say to me. What is his problem? Well, I don't
8　　　deserve to be treated like this. And you know what?
9　　　I'm going to end this before he does."
10　ISABEL: Heather broke up with Blake?
11　EMMA: About to.
12　ISABEL: Wow.
13　EMMA: *(Lowers voice.)* So, Isabel ... how do you feel about
14　　　me?
15　ISABEL: Why are you ... I mean, Blake, asking me this? It's
16　　　not like Blake is going to walk up to me and say,
17　　　*(Lowers voice)* "Isabel, how do you feel about me?"
18　EMMA: He might.
19　ISABEL: He might? Really?
20　EMMA: Uh-huh. It could happen.
21　ISABEL: Emma, why could it happen?
22　EMMA: Well, maybe because I told him my BFF had
23　　　something important to tell him.
24　ISABEL: Me? I'm supposed to have something important
25　　　to tell Blake? Why did you do that? And what
26　　　important thing am I supposed to have to say to
27　　　Blake?
28　EMMA: Don't worry about all that. Let's practice. *(Lowers*
29　　　*voice.)* "Isabel, what did you want to tell me?"
30　ISABEL: I hate you. You know it?
31　EMMA: Me or Blake?
32　ISABEL: You! Why would you tell Blake that I have
33　　　something important to tell him? We never talk.
34　　　Unless it's about him copying my notes or asking
35　　　about an assignment.

1 EMMA: Don't be upset. You'll thank me later.

2 ISABEL: *(Crosses arms.)* No I won't.

3 EMMA: *(Lowers voice.)* So what did you want to tell me?

4 ISABEL: Nothing.

5 EMMA: Isabel, come on!

6 ISABEL: Emma, this was your wonderful idea, not mine.

7   And I don't know what it is you think I need to say to

8   Blake. So maybe you need to tell me because when

9   that heartthrob walks up to me, I become tongue-

10   tied, so I wouldn't be able to say anything anyways.

11 EMMA: OK, OK. You be Blake and I'll be you.

12 ISABEL: No.

13 EMMA: Come on. Just humor me.

14 ISABEL: I'm not humored. Look at my face. Why are you

15   always having these great ideas that include me?

16 EMMA: What are friends for?

17 ISABEL: And I'm afraid this is just another great idea of

18   yours that turns out not to be so great.

19 EMMA: Come on, Isabel. Ask me how I feel about you.

20 ISABEL: And you're me?

21 EMMA: Yes.

22 ISABEL: And I'm Blake?

23 EMMA: Yes.

24 ISABEL: OK, fine. Just to put this all to an end, I'll play this

25   little game. *(Points finger at her.)* But you better watch

26   what you say. That is, watch what I say. *(As Blake)* So,

27   how do you feel about me?

28 EMMA: Can you lower your voice? It sounds more realistic

29   that way.

30 ISABEL: *(Reluctantly, she lowers her voice.)* Isabel, how do

31   you feel about me?

32 EMMA: *(Throws her arms around ISABEL.)* Oh, Blake. I love

33   you!

34 ISABEL: *(Prying EMMA off)* No! No way am I saying that.

35   Emma! Really? You think I could just throw my arms

1   around Blake and say I love him? I'd rather evaporate
2   into thin air.
3 EMMA: OK, OK. I suppose that was a little strong. Let's
4   start over. Say something. Anything.
5 ISABEL: I'm still Blake?
6 EMMA: Yes.
7 ISABEL: OK. *(Lowers voice.)* Hey.
8 EMMA: Hey, Blake. Listen, there is something I wanted to
9   tell you.
10 ISABEL: OK. What?
11 EMMA: It's about me ... well, and you.
12 ISABEL: Me and you?
13 EMMA: *(Twirls hair with finger.)* Uh-huh.
14 ISABEL: *(Slaps her hand.)* Stop! I wouldn't do that. *(Lowers*
15   *voice.)* What about me and you?
16 EMMA: Well, actually it's about my feelings about you.
17 ISABEL: Your feelings?
18 EMMA: Yes. Blake ...
19 ISABEL: Yeah?
20 EMMA: *(Throws arms around ISABEL.)* I love you!
21 ISABEL: *(Pries EMMA off.)* Emma! I'm not doing that.
22 EMMA: Sorry! Sorry! I got carried away again. Give me
23   one more chance, OK.
24 ISABEL: Last chance.
25 EMMA: OK. *(Pause)* I'm waiting.
26 ISABEL: *(Deep breath, aggravated. Lowers voice.)* Hey.
27 EMMA: Hey, Blake.
28 ISABEL: So what's up?
29 EMMA: Well, Blake, I wanted to talk to you.
30 ISABEL: *(Shrugs.)* OK. About what?
31 EMMA: Well, first of all I heard that things aren't going so
32   good for you and Heather.
33 ISABEL: Yeah. So?
34 EMMA: *(Twirls hair with finger.)* And I'm sorry. I'm really,
35   really sorry.

1 ISABEL: *(Slaps her hand.)* **Stop it! I wouldn't do that.**

2 **EMMA: Like I said, I'm really, really sorry.**

3 **ISABEL: Thanks.**

4 **EMMA: But maybe it's time for you both to move on.**

5 **ISABEL: Maybe.**

6 **EMMA: Move on to someone who appreciates your sense**

7   **of humor, your athletic ability, your crooked little**

8   **smile, and the way your eyes light up when you laugh.**

9 **ISABEL: Yeah, well ... that'd be nice to find someone like**

10   **that, I guess.**

11 **EMMA: And I know just that person, Blake.**

12 **ISABEL: You do?** *(Normal voice)* **Emma, I'm warning you ...**

13 **EMMA: It's me, Blake. Me!** *(Throws arms around EMMA.)* **I**

14   **love you, Blake!**

15 **ISABEL: I love you, too, Emma.**

16 **EMMA:** *(Steps away.)* **Not me. I'm you. You say I love you,**

17   **too, Isabel.**

18 **ISABEL: I say I love myself?**

19 **EMMA: Yes! Because you're not you, you're Blake. And I'm**

20   **not me, I'm you.**

21 **ISABEL:** *(Throws arms around EMMA.)* **I love you, Isabel!**

22   *(Pulls away.)* **That felt weird. To tell you I love myself.**

23 **EMMA: Wait! I'm Blake.**

24 **ISABEL: I'm confused.**

25 **EMMA: Well, anyway, you get the point don't you?**

26 **ISABEL: I get your point, but there is no way I could tell**

27   **Blake in real life that I love him. I'm not even sure if**

28   **I could tell Mr. Heartthrob that I like him.**

29 **EMMA: Yes you could.**

30 **ISABEL: No. Actually I'd rather die.**

31 **EMMA: No, you won't die. You need to tell Blake that you**

32   **like him and make it clear to him that you are**

33   **available. Very available.**

34 **ISABEL: I could never do that. Not in a million —**

35 **EMMA: Look! You're about to get your chance.**

1 **BLAKE:** *(Enters.)* **Hey.**

2 **EMMA: Hey.**

3 **ISABEL: Hey.**

4 **BLAKE: Isabel, you wanted to tell me something**
5   **important?**

6 **EMMA: Yes, she did.**

7 **ISABEL: I did?**

8 **EMMA:** *(Nudges ISABEL.)* **Yes you did.**

9 **ISABEL: Yes, I ... uh ... I ...** *(Suddenly)* **How's Heather?**

10 **BLAKE: We broke up.**

11 **EMMA: Yes!**

12 **BLAKE:** *(To EMMA)* **Yes?**

13 **EMMA: Yes ... I heard that and I wanted to tell you I was**
14   **sorry.**

15 **BLAKE: Oh.**

16 **ISABEL: I'm sorry, too.**

17 **BLAKE: Thanks. So what did you want to tell me, Isabel?**

18 **ISABEL: Well, I ... uh ...I ...**

19 **EMMA: She's struggling, Blake. Trying to find the right**
20   **words.**

21 **BLAKE: Just tell me, Isabel.**

22 **ISABEL: Well, I ... uh ... I ...**

23 **BLAKE: Yes?**

24 **EMMA:** *(Blurts out)* **She loves your crooked little smile.**

25 **BLAKE: You do?**

26 **ISABEL: Uh ... I ... uh ...**

27 **EMMA: And she loves your sense of humor.**

28 **BLAKE: You do?**

29 **ISABEL: Uh-huh.**

30 **EMMA: And your athletic ability.**

31 **BLAKE: Really?**

32 **ISABEL: Uh-huh.**

33 **EMMA: And she loves the way your eyes light up when you**
34   **laugh.**

35 **BLAKE: Wow. Thanks, Isabel. That was sweet.**

1   ISABEL: Well, I ... uh ...

2   BLAKE: Hey, maybe we could catch a movie tomorrow.

3   You think?

4   ISABEL: Me? You? Us?

5   EMMA: She'd love to, Blake.

6   BLAKE: Great. I'll call you tomorrow and we'll decide on

7   what movie to see. *(ISABEL nods.)* And thanks for

8   saying all those nice things about me. That was really

9   sweet. So you really like my crooked little smile?

10   *(Smiles at ISABEL. She nods.)* So, was there anything

11   else you wanted to tell me?

12 ISABEL: *(Throws her arms around BLAKE.)* I love you,

13   Blake!

24. Chatterbox

CAST: (1M, 2F) ERICA, MR. WILSON, JESSICA
PROPS: Book, piece of gum
SETTING: Classroom

1 *(At rise, ERICA is sitting at her desk at the front of the*
2 *class. MR. WILSON is at his desk nearby.)*
3 **ERICA: Mr. Wilson, I don't like sitting in front of the**
4 **classroom. Everyone is staring at me. Why are you**
5 **making me do this?**
6 **MR. WILSON: Talking.**
7 **ERICA: For asking to borrow a piece of notebook paper?**
8 **MR. WILSON: You're a little chatterbox, aren't you, Miss**
9 **Summers? You chat with those beside you, in front of**
10 **you, behind you, and even across the room. How am I**
11 **supposed to teach class with your nonstop visiting?**
12 **Well, now you have no one to talk to, do you?** *(He looks*
13 *down.)*
14 **ERICA:** *(Uses her hands and mouths the words to*
15 *communicate with a friend. She does not speak out loud.)*
16 **I can't believe I have to sit up here! Mr. Wilson is crazy!**
17 **MR. WILSON: No hand signing either, Miss Summers.**
18 **ERICA: What if I have something to say?**
19 **MR. WILSON: I suggest you keep it to yourself until after**
20 **class is over.**
21 **ERICA: But what if I have a question about our assignment?**
22 **MR. WILSON: Then you raise your hand and wait to be**
23 **called on.** *(ERICA raises her hand. MR. WILSON sees her,*
24 *but looks down and ignores her. She begins to waive her*
25 *hand wildly, making grunting sounds.)* **Yes, Erica?**
26 **ERICA: I don't understand question five.**
27 **MR. WILSON: Then read the book again and see if you can**
28 **figure it out on your own.**
29 **ERICA: You're not going to help me?**

1 MR. WILSON: I just did. I suggested you read the book ...
2   again.
3 ERICA: The whole book? But *Crime and Punishment* is
4   long. Five hundred and seventy-six pages!
5 MR. WILSON: Then you should be able to answer question
6   number five. What is the overall theme and meaning
7   of *Crime and Punishment?*
8 ERICA: Mr. Wilson, *Crime and Punishment* is far too
9   lengthy and complex to answer that question.
10 MR. WILSON: Then you better read it again.
11 ERICA: *(Looks back at her assignment, then raises her*
12   *hand.)* I have another question.
13 MR. WILSON: What?
14 ERICA: Number six. "Discuss Roskolnikov's theory of the
15   ordinary versus the extraordinary man."
16 MR. WILSON: What's your question?
17 ERICA: What does that mean?
18 MR. WILSON: What does the number six mean?
19 ERICA: Yes.
20 MR. WILSON: For crying out loud! It's pretty self-
21   explanatory if you ask me.
22 ERICA: I guess I'm having a hard time understanding the
23   book as a whole.
24 MR. WILSON: Class, is there anyone in here who can
25   summarize *Crime and Punishment* for Miss
26   Summers? Jessica? Come to the front please.
27 JESSICA: *(Enters and stands near MR. WILSON.)* Yes sir?
28 MR. WILSON: I assume you've read *Crime and*
29   *Punishment* as required for this class?
30 JESSICA: Yes sir.
31 MR. WILSON: Good. Then can you tell Miss Summers
32   about the book, please? Maybe it will jog some sort of
33   thought in her brain.
34 JESSICA: Yes sir. *Crime and Punishment* is a novel by
35   Russian author Fyodor Dostoyevsky.

1 ERICA: Who?

2 JESSICA: Fyodor Dostoyevsky. *Crime and Punishment* is a

3   major work of classical fiction. It was first published

4   in a literary journal in twelve-month installments in

5   1866. It was later published in book form in 1867.

6 ERICA: You sure know your facts, don't you?

7 JESSICA: The novel deals with several themes. Criminal

8   motivations, the human conscience, and conflict

9   with morality.

10 MR. WILSON: Thank you, Jessica.

11 JESSICA: You're welcome. *(Exits.)*

12 MR. WILSON: Does that help you, Miss Summers?

13 ERICA: Maybe for question number five. Overall theme

14   and meaning of *Crime and Punishment* ... *(Writes.)*

15   Several themes ... uh ... uh ... Jessica, can you tell me

16   those themes again? I need to write them down.

17   Criminal motivations and what?

18 MR. WILSON: Erica ...

19 ERICA: Yes sir?

20 MR. WILSON: Read the book!

21 ERICA: *(After a short pause)* Mr. Wilson?

22 MR. WILSON: What?

23 ERICA: Can I sit in my regular spot now?

24 MR. WILSON: No. You need to zip it and get to reading –

25   or answering those questions. *(Glances down.)*

26 ERICA: *(Mouths to one of her friends.)* I don't want to read

27   this stupid book! Why is he making me do this?

28 MR. WILSON: *(Watching her)* What did you just say?

29 JESSICA: *(From Off-Stage)* I know what she said. I can read

30   lips.

31 MR. WILSON: Come forward, Jessica.

32 JESSICA: *(Enters.)* She said, "I don't want to read this

33   stupid book! Why is he making mc do this?"

34 MR. WILSON: Thank you, Jessica. *(JESSICA exits.)* Miss

35   Summers, when I said no talking, it also meant this.

1   *(Moves his lips as if speaking)* **Got it?!**

2   **ERICA: Yes sir.**

3   **MR. WILSON: And none of this, either.** *(Does crazy hand*
4   *motions in air.)* **Got it?**

5   **ERICA: Yes sir.**

6   **MR. WILSON: All right, class, back to your assignment.**
7   *(Looks down.)*

8   **ERICA:** *(After a short pause)* **Mr. Wilson.**

9   **MR. WILSON: What?!**

10 **ERICA: Do you ever feel like you have so much inside of**
11   **you that you need to let it out?**

12 **MR. WILSON: No.**

13 **ERICA: Or that the silence of the room drives you crazy**
14   **and you can't think because it's so quiet?**

15 **MR. WILSON: No. I can't think when it's not quiet.**

16 **ERICA: Or that your life is just passing you by while you sit**
17   **in this classroom?**

18 **MR. WILSON: No.**

19 **ERICA: Or that you can't breathe if you're not allowed to**
20   **express your feelings?**

21 **MR. WILSON: No.**

22 **ERICA: Or lonely as the only sounds to be heard are the**
23   **ticking of the clock on the wall above your desk?**

24 **MR. WILSON: Those are not the sounds that I'm hearing.**
25   **Not the tick, tick, tick. But nails-on-the-chalkboard**
26   **chattering! What I'd like to hear are pages turning or**
27   **pens on paper.**

28 **ERICA: Mr. Wilson, do you hate your job?**

29 **MR. WILSON: Some days, I do.**

30 **ERICA: I would. I bet you count the minutes until the bell**
31   **rings at three-fifteen. I do. And did you really want to**
32   **be a teacher? Who'd want to go to school all of their**
33   **lives? And be forced to read a novel like *Crime and***
34   ***Punishment?* You actually chose to do this?**

35 **MR. WILSON: Miss Summers ...**

1   ERICA: Sir?

2   MR. WILSON: Shut up! Please. *(Short pause)*

3   ERICA: Mr. Wilson, I don't really like to read. Is the book

4   out on DVD? Maybe I can rent it and watch it instead.

5   MR. WILSON: Erica, for the last time ... be quiet!

6   ERICA: But what if I have a question to ask? Like number

7   seven?

8   MR. WILSON: Not now, Erica.

9   ERICA: Then when? When can I ask you a question about

10   number seven?

11   MR. WILSON: After class.

12   ERICA: But I can't stay after class. I have to hurry across

13   campus to the orchestra room.

14   MR. WILSON: Then email me your question later. I'll

15   respond to it by the following day.

16   ERICA: *(After a pause)* Mr. Wilson ...

17   MR. WILSON: *What?*

18   ERICA: Do you really like teaching?

19   MR. WILSON: No! No, I do not.

20   ERICA: I wouldn't either. *(Short pause)* Can I go to the

21   bathroom?

22   MR. WILSON: No.

23   ERICA: Get a drink of water?

24   MR. WILSON: No.

25   ERICA: Water your dying plant in the windowsill?

26   MR. WILSON: No.

27   ERICA: Sharpen your pencils?

28   MR. WILSON: No. I don't have any pencils.

29   ERICA: Which probably means you're really smart. Smart

30   people don't use pencils. Because they don't have to

31   erase. But that's all I use. Unless the teachers won't

32   let me. But most will.

33   MR. WILSON: Hush! Please. Just hush. Chew some gum or

34   something if that will help. But just hush!

35   ERICA: I thought we weren't allowed to chew gum in

36   class.

1 MR. WILSON: You're not. But if it will help you stop
2   talking, then go for it.
3 ERICA: Mr. Wilson ...
4 MR. WILSON: *What?*
5 ERICA: Can I borrow a piece of gum? *(MR. WILSON opens*
6   *his desk drawer, fumbles around, finds a piece of gum,*
7   *and slams it on ERICA's desk.)* Thank you. *(Chews the*
8   *gum. After a pause)* Mr. Wilson ...
9 MR. WILSON: *(Slams hand on desk.)* *What?*
10 ERICA: What kind of gum is this? I really like it. *(MR.*
11   *WILSON lays his head on his desk as if crying.)* Are you
12   all right? You know, I'd feel just like you if I had to
13   teach this same subject seven times a day. I bet it
14   drives you insane, doesn't it? And I bet you don't even
15   like *Crime and Punishment* either. Who'd want to
16   read this? It'd take me a year or two to get through it.
17   And that's not saying I'd even understand what I
18   read. I don't retain knowledge very well, you know.
19   Oh, and can we use cliff notes? *(MR. WILSON bangs*
20   *his head on the desk.)*

25. Extra Credit

CAST: (2M, 4F) FRANCIS, KATIE, MIKEY, SUSIE, LIBBY, SHAWN
PROPS: Notebook
SETTING: Kindergarten classroom

1   *(At rise, FRANCIS sits in a chair as kindergarten students*
2   *KATIE, MICKEY, SUSIE, LIBBY, and SHAWN sit on the*
3   *floor listening to her).*
4   **FRANCIS: Hi, kids. My name is Francis. I've come to your**
5   **class today to read you a story.**
6   **KATIE: Are you our new kindergarten teacher?**
7   **FRANCIS: No. I'm a student from Blackshear High School.**
8   **I've come to your class today to receive extra credit.**
9   **MIKEY: What's extra credit?**
10 **FRANCIS: Well, it's when you do something to get extra**
11   **points for a class.**
12 **SUSIE: Like this?** *(Jumps up and runs in place.)* **I'm working**
13   **hard, aren't I? Will I get extra credit?**
14 **FRANCIS: No, not like that. I take a creative writing class at**
15   **my school and we were asked to write a children's**
16   **story.**
17 **LIBBY: You're a writer?**
18 **FRANCIS: Well, sort of. My teacher wanted us to write a**
19   **story for children and that's what I have here.** *(Holds up*
20   *the notebook.)*
21 **SHAWN: What's it about? I hope it's about dinosaurs.** *(Gets*
22   *on his knees. Pulls on FRANCIS' arm.)* **Did you know**
23   **Tyrannosaurus Rex was the king of all dinosaurs?**
24   *(Growls as if he were a dinosaur.)* **And do you know what**
25   **they ate?**
26 **KATIE: Plants?**
27 **SHAWN: No! They ate other animals. Large animals.** *(Bends*
28   *over, makes a growling sound as if eating KATIE.)*

1   **KATIE: Stop it, Shawn.** *(To FRANCIS)* **Can you tell him to**
2   **stop it. I don't like dinosaurs.**
3   **MIKEY: I want to be a T. rex, too!** *(Makes growling sounds*
4   *and pretends to eat LIBBY.)*
5   **LIBBY: Stop it!**
6   **FRANCIS: OK boys, settle down. Now sit down and pay**
7   **attention.**
8   **SUSIE: Are you going to read us your story now?**
9   **MIKEY: I hope it's about dinosaurs.** *(Growls.)*
10   **SHAWN: Me, too.** *(Growls.)*
11   **SUSIE: I hope it's about unicorns.**
12   **LIBBY: Or ponies.**
13   **KATIE: Or princesses.**
14   **FRANCIS: My story is not about any of those things, but I**
15   **think you'll like it. OK, who wants to hear my story?**
16   *(They ALL raise their hands and say, "Me, me, me!"*
17   *FRANCIS opens notebook.)* **Once upon a time —**
18   **MICKEY:** *(Stands.)* **Can I get a drink of water?**
19   **SHAWN: Me too?**
20   **LIBBY: I'm thirsty too.**
21   **KATIE: I'm not. I want to hear the story.**
22   **SUSIE: I want to get a drink of water, too. Can I?**
23   **FRANCIS: No. Everyone sit down. My story is not that long.**
24   **MICKEY: Can I get a drink of water after your story?**
25   **SHAWN: And me too?**
26   **FRANCIS: We'll see.**
27   **LIBBY: Me, too.**
28   **SUSIE: And me.**
29   **FRANCIS: All right, everyone be quiet and listen to the**
30   **story.**
31   **MIKEY: You want us to zip our mouths?**
32   **SHAWN: That's what Miss Clements makes us do. Like**
33   **this!** *(Demonstrates. Through closed lips.)* **See! I zipped**
34   **my mouth.**
35   **FRANCIS: Yes. Why don't we all zip our mouths?**

1   KATIE: Except for you. Because then you couldn't talk.

2   FRANCIS: Everyone but me. Did everyone zip their
3   mouths? *(They ALL zip their mouths and nod.)* **Good.**
4   *(Looks at notebook.)* **Once upon a time there was a**
5   **caterpillar named Louie.**

6   MIKEY: I have an uncle named Louie.

7   LIBBY: Mikey, you were supposed to zip your mouth.

8   MIKEY: Well, you're talking, too.

9   LIBBY: No I'm not.

10   MIKEY: Yes you are.

11   FRANCIS: All right, let's zip our mouths one last time.
12   *(They ALL zip their mouths.)* **Louie was a very unusual**
13   **caterpillar.**

14   SUSIE: Why?

15   SHAWN: Let her read the story, Susie.

16   KATIE: They're talking again.

17   SHAWN: So are you.

18   LIBBY: I'm not.

19   MIKEY: Me neither.

20   FRANCIS: OK, zip! *(They ALL zip their mouths.)* **While**
21   **most caterpillars were green, Louie was a rainbow of**
22   **colors.**

23   KATIE: *(Claps.)* I like that! A rainbow caterpillar.

24   SHAWN: Caterpillars aren't the colors of a rainbow.

25   MIKEY: Yeah! That's stupid.

26   KATIE: *(Hits MIKEY.)* That's mean.

27   MIKEY: Ouch! *(Hits KATIE.)*

28   KATIE: Don't hit me.

29   MIKEY: You hit me first.

30   FRANCIS: All right, stop!

31   LIBBY: I'd like to see a rainbow caterpillar.

32   SUSIE: Me too.

33   FRANCIS: *(Reading)* **Louie was red, orange, yellow, green,**
34   **blue, and purple.**

35   KATIE: Ooooh! That sounds pretty. *(The other GIRLS nod.)*

1   SHAWN: You should've made him purple.

2   KATIE: He has purple on him.

3   SHAWN: No, all purple.

4   MIKEY: With red dots.

5   SHAWN: Yeah! That'd be cool.

6   MIKEY: Cooler than a rainbow caterpillar.

7   SUSIE: I like rainbow caterpillars.

8   SHAWN: But you've never seen one.

9   SUSIE: Yes I have.

10   MIKEY: No you haven't.

11   SUSIE: Uh-huh! *(Tugs at FRANCIS.)* Right? Because you've

12   seen them too, haven't you?

13   LIBBY: I saw one in my backyard yesterday. But my

14   brother went up to him and did this. *(Stands up and*

15   *stomps her foot.)*

16   SUSIE: Your brother killed the rainbow caterpillar?

17   LIBBY: Yes. My brother kills everything.

18   KATIE: Poor little caterpillar.

19   FRANCIS: Are you ready to hear the rest of the story? *(They*

20   *nod.)* Louie was red, orange, yellow, green, blue, and

21   purple. But sadly, the other caterpillars made fun of

22   Louie.

23   KATIE: They did?

24   LIBBY: Why?

25   SUSIE: Poor Louie.

26   SHAWN: *(Laughs.)* Because he looked funny.

27   SUSIE: Stop it, Shawn.

28   MIKEY: *(To SUSIE)* Like you. You look funny.

29   SUSIE: No I don't.

30   MIKEY: Yes you do.

31   SUSIE: *(Cries.)* No I don't.

32   LIBBY: No she doesn't! Susie, you're pretty.

33   MIKEY: I bet you wish you were the colors of a rainbow.

34   KATIE: Stop it, Mikey.

35   SHAWN: I want to be camouflage.

1 **MIKEY: Yeah.**

2 **FRANCIS: Does anyone want to hear my story?** *(They ALL*

3 *raise their hands.)* **So after being laughed at and**

4 **teased —**

5 **LIBBY:** *(To MIKEY)* **Like you're teasing Susie.** *(LIBBY and*

6 *KATIE put their arms around SUSIE.)*

7 **FRANCIS: Louie crawled underneath a big green leaf.**

8 **MIKEY: And ate it?** *(As if eating)* **Crunch, crunch, crunch!**

9 **SHAWN: Yeah!** *(As if eating)* **Crunch, crunch, crunch!**

10 **KATIE: Then what happened?**

11 **FRANCIS: Louie thought to himself, "I will hide**

12 **underneath here for the rest of my life."**

13 **KATIE: Why did he want to hide?**

14 **SHAWN: Because no one liked him.**

15 **SUSIE: I'd like him.**

16 **LIBBY: Me too. I'd tell him to come out and he could crawl**

17 **on my arm.**

18 **KATIE: Then what?**

19 **FRANCIS: Then one day, Louie felt something strange**

20 **happening.**

21 **MIKEY:** *(Raises hand.)* **I know! I know! I know!**

22 **SHAWN:** *(Raises hand.)* **Oh! I know, too! I know!**

23 **FRANCIS:** *(To MIKEY and SHAWN)* **Put your hands down**

24 **and listen to the story.**

25 **SUSIE: What happened?**

26 **MIKEY: He turned into a butterfly.**

27 **SHAWN: And flew away.**

28 **FRANCIS: Why didn't you just let me finish my story?**

29 **MIKEY:** *(Shrugs.)* **'Cause I knew that's what was going to**

30 **happen.**

31 **SHAWN: Me too!**

32 **FRANCIS: Louie transformed into a beautiful rainbow**

33 **butterfly.**

34 **MIKEY: See.**

35 **FRANCIS: And he was the most beautiful butterfly ever.**

1   LIBBY: And did he fly away?

2   KATIE: Far, far away and make new friends?

3   SUSIE: And he lived happily ever after.

4   LIBBY: The end.

5   MIKEY: Can I get a drink of water now? I'm thirsty.

6   SHAWN: Me too. I'm dying for a drink of water.

7   MIKEY: I'm dying for one, too.

8   FRANCIS: Sure. *(The BOYS run off.)*

9   SUSIE: I'm thirsty too!

10   KATIE: Me too!

11   LIBBY: So am I! *(The GIRLS run off.)*

12   FRANCIS: *(Looks at notebook.)* So Louie flew away. And

13   from that day on, everyone who saw Louie wanted to

14   be his friend. And he was never teased or felt lonely

15   again. Because now, Louie was the most beautiful

16   butterfly in the entire universe. And he lived happily

17   ever after. The end. *(She shuts the notebook.)*

26. Blind Date

CAST: (3M, 3F) DAVID, KAYLA, MONICA, JOEL, BELLA,
PETER
PROPS: Two coffee cups
SETTING: Coffee house

1   *(At rise, DAVID and KAYLA sit at a table drinking coffee.)*

2   **DAVID: Plain or peanut?**

3   **KAYLA: Plain. You?**

4   **DAVID: Peanut.**

5   **KAYLA: Winter or summer?**

6   **DAVID: Winter. You?**

7   **KAYLA: Summer.**

8   **DAVID: Dogs or cats?**

9   **KAYLA: Cats. I have two. You?**

10   **DAVID: Dogs. I have two also.**

11   **KAYLA: Well, that's the first thing we've had in common. We**

12   **both have two animals each.**

13   **DAVID: Do you like video games? Like Halo or Grand Theft**

14   **Auto?**

15   **KAYLA: Uh, no. But I like to make cupcakes. You would love**

16   **my cookie dough cupcakes. They are to die for.**

17   **DAVID: I'm not really into sweets. Sorry.**

18   **KAYLA: I guess you aren't into scrapbooking either, are you?**

19   **DAVID: No. Do you like to go deer hunting?**

20   **KAYLA: No. Jewelry-making?**

21   **DAVID: No. Fishing?**

22   **KAYLA: No. Shopping at the mall?**

23   **DAVID: I hate the mall. Do you like bowling?**

24   **KAYLA: Not really.** *(JOEL and MONICA enter.)*

25   **JOEL: Here they are.**

26   **MONICA: A match made in heaven. Don't you think, Joel?**

27   **JOEL: Could be, could be. Hey, sorry to interrupt your first**

28   **date, but since Monica and I set you two up, we wanted**

1   to see how it was going.

2 MONICA: And it's going great, isn't it? I can just tell by

3   looking at you two.

4 KAYLA: Well, we're definitely getting to know each other.

5   What the other likes and doesn't like.

6 DAVID: Right. Seeing how much we have in common.

7 MONICA: And I bet you have everything in common, don't

8   you?

9 DAVID: Well, actually —

10 MONICA: Like Joel and I! We are so much alike it's insane.

11 JOEL: That's right. Monica is just like me. Except she's

12   female.

13 MONICA: And he's like me. Except he's male.

14 JOEL: We both love action movies.

15 MONICA: And arcades.

16 JOEL: Chinese food.

17 MONICA: Auto racing sports.

18 JOEL: Nascar rocks!

19 MONICA: Biking.

20 JOEL: Hiking.

21 MONICA: Dancing.

22 JOEL: And peanut butter cookies!

23 MONICA: Oh yes! We both have our cravings for peanut

24   butter cookies. So, what do you two have in common?

25 DAVID: Well, actually —

26 JOEL: Do you want us to leave?

27 KAYLA: You don't have to.

28 JOEL: Monica, we probably shouldn't have barged in on

29   their first date.

30 MONICA: You're right. Sorry guys, but we just wanted to

31   stop by and say hello.

32 JOEL: And see how it was going.

33 MONICA: And it's going great, isn't it?

34 JOEL: And you two have everything in common, don't you?

35 MONICA: We knew it would work out. That's why Joel and

1   I set you up on this blind date. A perfect match.

2 JOEL: OK, we're leaving. Come on, Monica. Let's go.

3 MONICA: Sorry to interrupt.

4 JOEL: But we just wanted to say hello.

5 MONICA: And see how the blind date was going.

6 JOEL: Which apparently is going great.

7 MONICA: Oh, and you two look good together. Which I

8   think is important.

9 JOEL: Like us. We look good together, don't we? *(Puts his*

10   *arm around MONICA.)* Yes, we do. And so do you two.

11 MONICA: We should go.

12 JOEL: I agree. Let's leave these two lovebirds alone so they

13   can continue to find all the reasons they belong

14   together.

15 MONICA: And I bet there are a million reasons why.

16 JOEL: What's that saying?

17 MONICA: Two peas in a pod.

18 JOEL: That's them.

19 MONICA: And us! A perfect match. OK, OK, we're leaving.

20   *(To KAYLA)* Call me later. I want to hear everything.

21 JOEL: *(To DAVID)* Catch you later, man. Bye.

22 MONICA: Bye. *(JOEL and MONICA exit.)*

23 DAVID: Wow.

24 KAYLA: All I can say is their intentions were good.

25 DAVID: Yes. You can't blame them for trying.

26 KAYLA: True.

27 DAVID: OK, I have another one.

28 KAYLA: OK.

29 DAVID: Sweet or salty?

30 KAYLA: Sweet. You?

31 DAVID: Salty.

32 KAYLA: Fried or scrambled?

33 DAVID: Fried. You?

34 KAYLA: Scrambled.

35 DAVID: White or wheat?

1   **KAYLA: Wheat. You?**

2   **DAVID: White.**

3   **KAYLA: David, we are complete opposites. Why did Joel**
4   **and Monica think that we were perfect for each**
5   **other?**

6   **DAVID: I don't know, Kayla. Except maybe as their friends**
7   **they wanted to see us both as happy as they are.**

8   **KAYLA: I guess.**

9   **DAVID: And like you said, their intentions were good.**

10 **KAYLA: True.**

11 **DAVID: Morning person?**

12 **KAYLA: Night. You?**

13 **DAVID: Morning.**

14 **KAYLA: Beach or mountains?**

15 **DAVID: Mountains. You?**

16 **KAYLA: Beach.**

17 **DAVID: Read or watch TV?**

18 **KAYLA: Read. You?**

19 **DAVID: TV.** *(PETER and BELLA enter.)*

20 **PETER: Hey, guys. What's happening?**

21 **BELLA: We just heard a rumor about you two.**

22 **PETER: You're on a blind date!**

23 **BELLA:** *(Offers her hand to KAYLA.)* **I'm Bella. I heard you**
24   **recently moved next door to Monica.**

25 **KAYLA: That's right.**

26 **BELLA: Well, it's nice to meet you.**

27 **PETER:** *(Offers his hand to KAYLA.)* **And I'm Peter. Bella's**
28   **boyfriend.**

29 **KAYLA: Nice to meet you both.**

30 **BELLA: Well, we just heard that this has the potential for**
31   **a love story in the making.**

32 **PETER: That's right. We just ran into Joel and Monica.**

33 **BELLA: And I can see the connection you two have. It's so**
34   **obvious.**

35 **DAVID: It is?**

1 BELLA: Yes! You know, some people just look like they
2   belong together.
3 PETER: And you two look like you belong together.
4 BELLA: Like Peter and I.
5 PETER: Yes! Like Bella and I. So, have you been talking
6   nonstop? Can't believe how much you both have in
7   common?
8 KAYLA: Well, actually —
9 PETER: Man, I hate blind dates.
10 BELLA: *(To PETER)* And just how many blind dates have
11   you been on?
12 PETER: Only a couple before meeting you, my love.
13 BELLA: And?
14 PETER: And they were a disaster! I couldn't wait for the
15   date to end. Misery. Pure misery.
16 BELLA: Oh ... you poor baby!
17 PETER: But I'm glad we found each other.
18 KAYLA: Where did you two meet?
19 BELLA: Home room.
20 PETER: My favorite class of the day. First period. Seeing
21   you.
22 BELLA: Mine too. And we've been together ever since.
23 PETER: *(To DAVID and KAYLA)* So, it's going great, huh?
24 DAVID: Well, actually —
25 BELLA: Have you made plans to see each other again?
26 KAYLA: Not yet.
27 PETER: We can help you with that. Since this whole blind
28   date thing is awkward in itself. How about dinner
29   and a movie tomorrow night?
30 BELLA: Yes! He can pick you up at six o'clock.
31 PETER: And David knows where you live since you live
32   next door to Monica.
33 BELLA: And ... if you're not quite ready for a real date we
34   can double.
35 PETER: No, triple date! With Joel and Monica.

1   BELLA: Peter, that's a great idea. So you two guys show up
2   at Monica's house at six o'clock and pick us up.
3   PETER: It's a plan.
4   BELLA: A date.
5   PETER: A triple date.
6   BELLA: When I get home I'll call Monica and let her know
7   our plans. She'll love it.
8   PETER: Great. OK, see you guys tomorrow. Bye.
9   BELLA: Bye! *(PETER and BELLA exit.)*
10 DAVID: That was awkward.
11 KAYLA: Everyone sure does want this to work out.
12 DAVID: I wonder why?
13 KAYLA: I guess to say they were a part of putting
14   something good together.
15 DAVID: Too bad we're not a match.
16 KAYLA: Nothing in common.
17 DAVID: Opposites in every way possible.
18 KAYLA: But you know ...
19 DAVID: What?
20 KAYLA: There is that saying.
21 DAVID: What saying?
22 KAYLA: Opposites attract.
23 DAVID: Are you attracted to me?
24 KAYLA: I am.
25 DAVID: And I'm attracted to you. You know, maybe it
26   would be more fun and interesting to date someone
27   who's different. Who shows you the other side of
28   things?
29 KAYLA: I like summer, but you could show me the reasons
30   to love winter.
31 DAVID: Cuddling. *(KAYLA smiles.)* And I like salty, but you
32   could introduce me to some of your favorite sweets.
33   Like cupcakes.
34 KAYLA: You would love them.
35 DAVID: I bet I would. And you know what? I think it'd be

1   boring to be with someone who liked everything you
2   liked. Did everything you did. How can you
3   experience new adventures, like cookie dough
4   cupcakes, if you're not willing to grow?
5   KAYLA: I agree.
6   DAVID: Hey, we finally have something in common.
7   KAYLA: What's that?
8   DAVID: We both agree that opposites attract.

27. The Happy Song

CAST: (2F) MANDY, JOANIE
SETTING: Waiting room at the doctor's office

1 *(At rise, MANDY and JOANIE are sitting next to each*
2 *other.)*
3 **MANDY:** *(Sneezes. To JOANIE)* **I'm not contagious.**
4 **JOANIE: We're at a doctor's office. I'd think everyone here is**
5 **contagious.**
6 **MANDY: It's allergies. I need a shot and some meds.**
7 **JOANIE: What are you allergic to?**
8 **MANDY: My cats. I have six of them.**
9 **JOANIE: Get rid of them.**
10 **MANDY: No! I love them. They're my babies. There's Felix,**
11 **Jasper, Gabby, Tiger, Harley, and Salina.**
12 **JOANIE: I don't like cats. Or animals.**
13 **MANDY: I see. So, what are you here for? If you don't mind**
14 **me asking.**
15 **JOANIE: Depression.**
16 **MANDY: That's not contagious either. So I guess it's good we**
17 **sat next to each other.**
18 **JOANIE: True. And as crowded as it is in here, it looks like**
19 **it's going to be a long wait.**
20 **MANDY: I hate going to the doctor.**
21 **JOANIE: Me too.**
22 **MANDY:** *(Sneezes.)* **Excuse me. So ... you're depressed?**
23 **JOANIE: Yes.**
24 **MANDY: About what?**
25 **JOANIE: Life.**
26 **MANDY: Life in general? Nothing specific?**
27 **JOANIE: I guess I could get specific. I hate my job. I have no**
28 **friends.**
29 **MANDY: And no pets.**
30 **JOANIE: No pets. No boyfriend. And my favorite TV show**

1   was just cancelled and now I'm wondering what I

2   have to live for.

3 MANDY: It sounds like you need a new outlook on life.

4 JOANIE: I guess.

5 MANDY: And prescriptions could work, but wouldn't you

6   like to try something else first?

7 JOANIE: Like what?

8 MANDY: Changing your attitude.

9 JOANIE: Sure, but I don't know how.

10 MANDY: I can help you.

11 JOANIE: How?

12 MANDY: *(Offers her hand.)* I'm Mandy, your new friend.

13 JOANIE: Thanks. I'm Joanie. But you don't even know me.

14 MANDY: *(Sneezes.)* Doesn't matter. So, what do you like to

15   do for fun?

16 JOANIE: Watch TV mostly.

17 MANDY: Besides that?

18 JOANIE: Scratch lottery cards. But I always lose.

19 MANDY: Do you like to go dancing?

20 JOANIE: I might, but I don't know how.

21 MANDY: *(Claps hands.)* Great! Then I'm the one to teach

22   you.

23 JOANIE: You'd do that?

24 MANDY: Sure. *(Stands and does a little dance.)* I'm a great

25   dancer.

26 JOANIE: Uh ... I wouldn't do that in here.

27 MANDY: Oh who cares? Most everyone is sleeping or

28   staring at magazines. Look at this move. *(Another*

29   *dance move)* Think you could do that?

30 JOANIE: Maybe.

31 MANDY: Stand up and try it. No one's looking.

32 JOANIE: *(Stands, but dances very badly.)* Like this?

33 MANDY: *(Helping)* Move your hips a little more like this.

34   That's right. Yeah! That's good.

35 JOANIE: You think I'm good? I've always wanted to go

1   dancing. But I just don't know how.

2   **MANDY:** Joanie, I can teach you a million moves. And this

3   weekend you could go dancing with me and my

4   friends. They'd love you. And my friend Jason has

5   been feeling down after Ashley broke his heart, so

6   he'd enjoy meeting someone new.

7   **JOANIE:** But I don't really like crowds.

8   **MANDY:** You can just get over that.

9   **JOANIE:** I'd like to.

10   **MANDY:** Are you still feeling depressed?

11   **JOANIE:** Unfortunately yes.

12   **MANDY:** Well, you have a new friend. You've learned a new

13   dance move. And you're going out dancing with

14   friends this weekend. All that is something to get

15   excited about.

16   **JOANIE:** What if they don't like me?

17   **MANDY:** They'll love you.

18   **JOANIE:** I don't know.

19   **MANDY:** I know. We need to sing a happy song.

20   **JOANIE:** *(Looking around)* In here?

21   **MANDY:** You've got to quit worrying about what other

22   people think. We don't know them so who cares?

23   **JOANIE:** But I've always been a bit on the shy side. And I do

24   worry about what other people think. Especially

25   about me.

26   **MANDY:** Oh, pooh! Forget about all those people out there.

27   They don't know you, you don't know them, so who

28   the heck gives a flip? Besides, they're probably too

29   sick to care about anything else right now.

30   **JOANIE:** OK, I'll try.

31   **MANDY:** Happy song! "If you're happy and you know it, clap

32   your hands!" *(Claps.)* "If you're happy and you know it,

33   clap your hands!" *(Claps.)* "If you're happy and you know

34   it, then your face will surely show it, if you're happy and

35   you know it, clap your hands!" *(Claps.)*

1   JOANIE: Isn't that a preschool song?

2   MANDY: Who cares? It's a happy song! Come on, you try it.

3   JOANIE: OK. *(Sings quietly and without emotion.)* "If you're

4   happy and you know it, clap your hands." *(Claps.)*

5   MANDY: Oh, Joanie, you can do better than that.

6   JOANIE: I'm sorry. I'm trying. But I'm depressed.

7   MANDY: Try this. *(Stands up and swings her hips wildly as*

8   *she sings and claps.)* "If you're happy and you know it,

9   clap your hands!" *(Claps.)* "If you're happy and you

10   know it, clap your hands!" *(Claps.)* "If you're happy

11   and you know it, then your face will surely show it, if

12   you're happy and you know it, clap your hands!"

13   *(Claps.)* Come on. You can do it. It's such a happy song

14   that you can't help but feel happy when you sing it.

15 JOANIE: But I'm not feeling very happy. I'm sad.

16 MANDY: Stop saying that. Say this. I'm happy.

17 JOANIE: *(Dryly)* I'm happy.

18 MANDY: Good. Now smile when you say it. I'm happy!

19 JOANIE: *(Half smile)* I'm happy.

20 MANDY: Excellent! Now aren't you feeling better?

21 JOANIE: A little.

22 MANDY: Now do this. *(Throws arms in the air.)* I'm happy!

23 JOANIE: *(Raises her arms without emotion.)* I'm happy.

24 MANDY: Now feel it! Feel it when you say it. *(Throws arms*

25   *in the air.)* I'm happy! I'm so happy!

26 JOANIE: *(Arms in air.)* I'm happy. I'm happy. I'm so, so

27   happy. *(To MANDY)* You know, I think this is working.

28   I'm happy. I'm happy. I'm so happy!

29 MANDY: See. It's just a change of attitude.

30 JOANIE: *(Throws arms in air.)* I'm happy!

31 MANDY: And you're not feeling as depressed anymore, are

32   you?

33 JOANIE: *(Jumps up.)* No. *(Throws arms in air.)* I'm happy!

34 MANDY: *(Gives her a hug.)* That is wonderful! *(Sneezes.)*

35   And I'm so happy for you.

1 JOANIE: I don't need to see a doctor anymore. Because I'm
2   not depressed. I was in a rut. I needed to get out. I
3   needed to meet people.
4 MANDY: And go dancing this weekend.
5 JOANIE: *(Swings hips wildly.)* Dancing this weekend.
6 MANDY: Meeting my friend, Jason.
7 JOANIE: *(Swings hips.)* Meeting your friend, Jason. Hel-lo,
8   Jason.
9 MANDY: *(Waves.)* Good-bye, depression!
10 JOANIE: *(Swings hips.)* Good-bye, feeling crummy and sad.
11   Hel-lo Jason!
12 MANDY: "If you're happy and you know it, clap your
13   hands!"
14 JOANIE and MANDY: *(Both clap.)* "If you're happy and you
15   know it, clap your hands! If you're happy and you
16   know it, clap your hands! If you're happy and you
17   know it, then your face will surely show it, if you're
18   happy and you know it, clap your hands!" *(Both clap.)*

28. Teen Movie Star

CAST: (1M, 6F) CHESTER, LILLY, COURTNEY, SIERRA, BECKY, MRS. SANDERS, MRS. SHORE
PROPS: Five pair of sunglasses, purses or backpacks for the girls, piece of paper, pen, bottle of eye drops
SETTING: School hallway

1   *(At rise, CHESTER enters wearing sunglasses. He pushes*
2   *his hair back and then leans against the wall. LILLY,*
3   *COURTNEY, and SIERRA, who are standing across the*
4   *hall, are watching him.)*
5   **LILLY: Who is that?**
6   **COURTNEY: I don't know. I've never seen him before.**
7   **SIERRA: He must think he's all that wearing his sunglasses**
8   **inside the school building.**
9   **COURTNEY: Maybe he is all that.**
10   **LILLY: Maybe he's a new student.**
11   **SIERRA: A teen movie star in disguise?**
12   **LILLY: Maybe he's protecting his identity while he tries to**
13   **live a normal life. You know, attending high school.**
14   **COURTNEY: Look how he pushes his hair back. He doesn't**
15   **look like any of the other boys around here.**
16   **SIERRA: He does look like a movie star with those**
17   **sunglasses on.**
18   **BECKY:** *(Enters.)* **What is everyone staring at?**
19   **LILLY:** *(Pointing)* **Him.**
20   **BECKY: Who is that in the sunglasses? Is he a new student?**
21   **COURTNEY: We were wondering that ourselves.**
22   **SIERRA: I think he's trying to hide his identity.**
23   **LILLY: Because he's famous.**
24   **BECKY: Maybe. Who else gets away with wearing sunglasses**
25   **at school?**
26   **COURTNEY: No one.**
27   **SIERRA: Unless they've changed the school policy.**

1 **BECKY: Well, let's see. Let's put on our sunglasses.** *(GIRLS*
2 *take out their sunglasses and put them on.)*
3 **LILLY: Looking cool at school.**
4 **SIERRA: Yes we are.**
5 **COURTNEY: If they have changed the school policy, I**
6 **might wear mine all the time. Don't I look good in my**
7 **shades?**
8 **BECKY: You do.**
9 **LILLY: But it is a little dark.**
10 **SIERRA: Which means you could sleep during class.**
11 **COURTNEY: Oh, I like that.**
12 **LILLY: Me too.**
13 **BECKY: Look. Here comes Mrs. Sanders. Everyone look at**
14 **her and smile as she walks by. If she says nothing**
15 **about us wearing the sunglasses, then that means the**
16 **school policy has changed.**
17 **SIERRA: And it also means that guy standing over there**
18 **against the wall is no one special.**
19 **MRS. SANDERS:** *(Enters.)* **Girls, what do you think you're**
20 **doing?**
21 **BECKY: What do you mean, Mrs. Sanders?**
22 **LILLY: Is something wrong?**
23 **COURTNEY: We're just talking. Lunch is over and we're**
24 **waiting for the bell to ring.**
25 **MRS. SANDERS: Take those sunglasses off right now.**
26 **BECKY: We can't wear them?**
27 **MRS. SANDERS: Absolutely not. Sunglasses are not**
28 **permitted inside the school building. So take them**
29 **off right now.** *(The GIRLS take off the glasses.)* **And**
30 **don't let me see you with them on again.**
31 **GIRLS: Yes ma'am.** *(MRS. SANDERS walks over to*
32 *CHESTER. The girls watch closely.)*
33 **BECKY: Now let's see if Mrs. Sanders makes that wannabe**
34 **movie star take off his shades.**
35 **SIERRA: I'm sure she will.**

1   **LILLY: Of course she will.**

2   **COURTNEY: She has to.**

3   **MRS. SANDERS:** *(To CHESTER)* **Hi. How are you?**

4   **CHESTER: Good.**

5   **MRS. SANDERS: Well, that's just wonderful. Oh, I meant**

6   **to ask you. Could you sign this for me?**

7   **CHESTER: Sure.**

8   **SIERRA: Look! Mrs. Sanders is asking for his autograph.**

9   **LILLY: I can't believe this.**

10   **MRS. SANDERS:** *(To CHESTER)* **Thank you. Thank you so**

11   **much! I hope you have a great day!**

12   **CHESTER: You too.** *(Pushes his hair back then leans against*

13   *the wall.)*

14   **BECKY: Mrs. Sanders didn't tell him to remove his**

15   **sunglasses.**

16   **COURTNEY: Which means he is trying to hide his identity.**

17   **LILLY: And the teachers at school are all in on it.**

18   **SIERRA: They have to be.**

19   **BECKY: Which means ...**

20   **SIERRA: He's a movie star!**

21   **COURTNEY: I wish he'd take off his sunglasses so I could**

22   **get a better look.**

23   **LILLY: I know. But even with the sunglasses on he looks**

24   **amazing.**

25   **SIERRA: I'd like to get his autograph.**

26   **BECKY: Me too. Whoever he is.**

27   **LILLY: Look. Mrs. Shore is headed this way. Let's try**

28   **wearing our sunglasses one more time. Just to make**

29   **sure.**

30   **BECKY: Good idea.** *(The GIRLS put on their sunglasses.)*

31   **MRS. SHORE:** *(Enters and approaches the girls.)* **What is**

32   **this?**

33   **COURTNEY: What?**

34   **SIERRA: What are you talking about, Mrs. Shore?**

35   **MRS. SHORE:** *(Waving her hand)* **This!**

1 LILLY: Waiting for the bell to ring?

2 MRS. SHORE: *(Waving her hand)* No, this.

3 BECKY: This lipstick color? It's shimmery pale pink. Do

4   you like it? Do you want to try it? You can borrow

5   mine.

6 MRS. SHORE: Not the lipstick. The sunglasses.

7 COURTNEY: It's the style, Mrs. Shore.

8 SIERRA: A way to look cool. In or out of the classroom.

9 LILLY: And don't we look cool?

10 BECKY: Or maybe look like we're someone famous?

11 MRS. SHORE: Take them off right now.

12 BECKY: But —

13 MRS. SHORE: *Now. (The GIRLS remove their sunglasses.)*

14   Give them to me.

15 COURTNEY: Why?

16 LILLY: We took them off like you said.

17 MRS. SHORE: Give them to me. *(The GIRLS hand her the*

18   *sunglasses.)* You all know good and well that

19   sunglasses are not permitted inside the school

20   building. You may go to the office at the end of the

21   day and collect them. For five dollars each.

22 SIERRA: Five dollars?

23 MRS. SHORE: And next time I catch you girls with these

24   on, they will be deposited into the dumpster.

25   Understand?

26 GIRLS: Yes ma'am. *(MRS. SHORE walks over to CHESTER.)*

27 BECKY: OK, let's see what Mrs. Shore has to say to the

28   movie star in question.

29 LILLY: I bet she takes his sunglasses away too.

30 COURTNEY: She has to. *(The GIRLS watch MRS. SHORE.)*

31 MRS. SHORE: *(To CHESTER)* Hello! *(Hand on his shoulder)*

32   Are you getting around OK?

33 CHESTER: So far, so good.

34 MRS. SHORE: I'm so glad to hear that! And if there's

35   anything you need, you just let me know. *(Giggles.)* An

1   escort to class, help with homework ... anything you
2   need. Anything at all.
3 CHESTER: Thanks. I appreciate it. *(MRS. SHORE exits.)*
4 SIERRA: I don't believe it! Mrs. Shore didn't make him
5   hand over his sunglasses.
6 LILLY: Or threaten to dispose of them in the dumpster.
7 COURTNEY: No. She offered to escort him to class or help
8   him with his homework.
9 BECKY: I'm surprised she didn't ask him for his
10   autograph.
11 LILLY: Probably because she has him as a student and will
12   get his autograph every single day.
13 SIERRA: Right. And she'll probably cut the heading off
14   the top of his assignments so she can auction them
15   off on eBay.
16 BECKY: Oh! I'm dying to know who that is.
17 COURTNEY: Me too.
18 LILLY: And he's so cute. Don't you think he's cute?
19 SIERRA: Yes! And I love it when he pushes his hair back
20   like this. *(Demonstrates.)*
21 BECKY: Wow. He's so hot.
22 COURTNEY: Let me at him.
23 LILLY: No, let me at him.
24 BECKY: So, why don't we go over there?
25 SIERRA: And do what?
26 BECKY: Just act nonchalant. As if we don't know or care
27   who he is.
28 COURTNEY: Yeah. And then we could bring up a casual
29   subject to talk about. Like the weather.
30 LILLY: And then maybe when he speaks, we'll be able to
31   figure out who he is.
32 BECKY: Then maybe we can offer to help him with his
33   homework.
34 SIERRA: I would.
35 LILLY: Me too.

1   COURTNEY: Here's my number, Mr. Teen Movie Star. Call
2   me sometime.
3   LILLY: So we're going to do it?
4   BECKY: Let's do it. Now listen, we'll walk over there while
5   talking about random stuff then just stop right next
6   to him. But don't look at him yet. We want him to
7   think we're not going over there on purpose.
8   SIERRA: Good idea.
9   LILLY: Let's go. *(The GIRLS walk over to CHESTER, laughing*
10   *and talking about school.)*
11   COURTNEY: Has anyone finished those Civil War
12   questions that Mr. Hopkins handed out?
13   LILLY: Not me.
14   SIERRA: I'm only halfway through. It's a pain.
15   COURTNEY: Due tomorrow.
16   LILLY: Oh, great.
17   BECKY: *(Looking toward CHESTER, then back to the other*
18   *girls.)* Man, is it ever hot.
19   SIERRA: It sure is hot.
20   LILLY: I heard it might reach a hundred today.
21   COURTNEY: That is hot.
22   BECKY: *(Looking at CHESTER)* Yes, very hot. Very, very hot!
23   SIERRA: I agree.
24   LILLY: Yes, I feel the temperature rising.
25   BECKY: *(To CHESTER)* Do you like the hot weather?
26   CHESTER: It's OK. *(The GIRLS look at each other wondering*
27   *what to say next.)*
28   COURTNEY: Nice sunglasses.
29   CHESTER: Thanks.
30   SIERRA: The teachers wouldn't let us wear ours.
31   LILLY: School policy.
32   BECKY: But I guess they made an exception for you.
33   CHESTER: Yeah. *(The GIRLS look at each other wondering*
34   *what to say next.)*
35   BECKY: *(To CHESTER)* You know, you could call me

1   **sometime if you ever needed any help finding your**
2   **way around.** *(Writes down her phone number for him.)*
3 **COURTNEY: Me too! Call me anytime.** *(To BECKY)* **Can I**
4   **borrow that pen and paper?** *(Writes down her phone*
5   *number for him.)*
6 **SIERRA: And you could call me if you ever needed any**
7   **homework help. I make pretty good grades.** *(To*
8   *COURTNEY)* **Hand me that pen and paper.** *(Writes*
9   *down her phone number for him.)*
10 **LILLY: Or if you need to know the hot spots around town,**
11   **give me a call.** *(To SIERRA)* **I need that pen and paper**
12   **now.** *(Writes down her phone number for him.)*
13 **CHESTER:** *(Takes the piece of paper with their phone*
14   *numbers.)* **Thanks.**
15 **LILLY: Anytime.**
16 **SIERRA: Day or night.**
17 **COURTNEY: Night or day.**
18 **BECKY: Twenty-four-seven. I'm here.**
19 **CHESTER: Wow. Thanks.**
20 **BECKY: So ... I'm curious.**
21 **CHESTER: About what?**
22 **BECKY: Your name.**
23 **CHESTER: You don't know?**
24 **BECKY: No.**
25 **CHESTER: Oh. It's Chester Malone.**
26 **BECKY: Who?**
27 **CHESTER: Chester.**
28 **BECKY: Chester who?**
29 **CHESTER: Malone. Don't you recognize me?**
30 **BECKY: No.**
31 **SIERRA: I don't either.**
32 **COURTNEY: Me neither.**
33 **LILLY: That name kind of sounds familiar. But from**
34   **what? What movie?**
35 **CHESTER:** *(Takes off the sunglasses.)* **It's me! Chester Malone.**

1 LILLY: That Chester Malone who slouches in the chair in
2   front of me in English class?
3 CHESTER: It's me.
4 SIERRA: The Chester Malone who likes to make snorting
5   sounds in band.
6 CHESTER: *(Laughs.)* Yeah! That's me. *(Snorts.)*
7 COURTNEY: Who hangs out with Larry Monroe and Leroy
8   Pendergrass?
9 CHESTER: *(Laughs.)* That's me!
10 BECKY: Then why are you standing over here pretending
11   to be all that?
12 COURTNEY: And why are the teachers letting you wear
13   sunglasses to school?
14 LILLY: Yeah! Why Chester Malone?
15 CHESTER: Because I had minor eye surgery yesterday.
16 SIERRA: What?
17 CHESTER: The optometrist said I had to wear sunglasses
18   for the next few days. I also have to put drops in my
19   eyes three times a day. I probably need to do that
20   right now. *(Tilts head and puts drops in eyes.)*
21 COURTNEY: That's why the teachers are letting you wear
22   sunglasses?
23 LILLY: And offering to help you around school and with
24   your homework assignments?
25 CHESTER: Uh-huh. Nice isn't it? *(Snorts.)*
26 SIERRA: But why did Mrs. Sanders ask you for your
27   autograph?
28 CHESTER: Oh, that. That was a form she needed me to
29   sign so I could be dismissed from physical education
30   this week. Mrs. Sanders didn't think I needed to be
31   outside in the hot sun. Even with my sunglasses on.
32 BECKY: So you're a nobody?
33 COURTNEY: A wannabe?
34 SIERRA: A fake?
35 CHESTER: *(Laughs.)* No. I'm Chester Malone. *(Snorts.)*

1   **Remember? I have some of you girls in my classes.**

2   **That's funny you forgot who I was.** *(Holds up the*

3   *phone numbers.)* **And thanks for the phone numbers.**

4   **I'll be calling each and every one of you. Day or night.**

5   **Night or day. Twenty-four-seven!** *(As he starts to exit)*

6   **Yes!** *(Snorts. The GIRLS look at each other and moan.)*

29. Teacher's Assistant

CAST: (2M, 3F) MRS. STONE, MADDIE, GARRETT, JOSH, HAILEY
PROPS: Hair clip, paper, pens, red pen, grade book
SETTING: Classroom

1   MRS. STONE: Maddie, thank you for coming by early this
2   morning to introduce yourself to me. I'm thrilled you
3   are going to be my teacher's assistant for third period.
4   Are you new to Cooper High? I don't usually get an
5   assistant during the middle of a semester.
6   MADDIE: No ma'am. I was in theatre class, but it just wasn't
7   working out for me.
8   MRS. STONE: What happened?
9   MADDIE: Apparently I'm too eager or dramatic or
10   something. Mr. Tatum was always telling me to bring it
11   down a notch.
12   MRS. STONE: Well, it's good you're such a little go-getter.
13   Because that's exactly what I need.
14   MADDIE: Thank you. Mr. Tatum said to come back to drama
15   next year if I wanted. When I figured out how to bring
16   it down a few notches.
17   MRS. STONE: That seems odd.
18   MADDIE: That's what I thought. Shouldn't people in drama
19   be dramatic?
20   MRS. STONE: You'd think so.
21   MADDIE: Oh well.
22   MRS. STONE: Actually Maddie, being my teacher's assistant
23   might just be the job for you.
24   MADDIE: Why do you say that?
25   MRS. STONE: Because you're good at drama.
26   MADDIE: I think so. Mr. Tatum thinks I'm over the top or
27   something.
28   MRS. STONE: Well, I need someone who can reach down
29   deep inside and command authority.

1   MADDIE: I'm sure I can do that.
2   MRS. STONE: Do you know many of the eighth grade
3   students?
4   MADDIE: No ma'am. Eighth graders are a little below me,
5   if you know what I mean.
6   MRS. STONE: Perfect!
7   MADDIE: Why do you ask?
8   MRS. STONE: Maddie, I want you to step in and teach my
9   third period class for me.
10 MADDIE: You do?
11 MRS. STONE: Yes.
12 MADDIE: Where will you be?
13 MRS. STONE: The teacher's lounge. My favorite soap
14   opera comes on during third period and I don't want
15   to miss an episode.
16 MADDIE: And you're going to let me teach your class?
17 MRS. STONE: If you'll agree.
18 MADDIE: Sure. This could be fun.
19 MRS. STONE: Great! I suggest you throw your hair up in a
20   clip and tell my eighth graders you look young for
21   your age.
22 MADDIE: I can do that.
23 MRS. STONE: I know you can, Maddie. I have all my faith
24   in you. I will leave the daily assignments on my desk
25   for you and all you have to do is tell the students what
26   to do and keep the class under control.
27 MADDIE: Sounds easy enough to me.
28 MRS. STONE: And this is perfect timing because Lazarus's
29   ex-wife has kidnapped Cassie. And she's holding her
30   in a dungeon.
31 MADDIE: Cassie? Lazarus? Who are they?
32 MRS. STONE: On my soap opera.
33 MADDIE: Oh.
34 MRS. STONE: So anyway, this is going to work out great.
35   And by the way, I mostly hand out word searches and

1   crossword puzzles to the students each day. So you
2   just have to hand them out, then you can kick back at
3   my desk and relax. Easy as pie.
4 MADDIE: So I'm the third period teacher?
5 MRS. STONE: Yes you are. And don't forget to clip your
6   hair back. I think it'll be more convincing if you
7   appear a little older. You know what I mean? Here. I
8   have an extra hair clip right here. Do you want to try
9   it out?
10 MADDIE: Sure. *(Clips her hair back.)*
11 MRS. STONE: Perfect! You look like you're in your early
12   twenties.
13 MADDIE: *(Likes this.)* I do?
14 MRS. STONE: You do.
15 MADDIE: One question, Mrs. Stone. What if the students
16   ask for help on the assignments? And what if I don't
17   know the answers?
18 MRS. STONE: That's easy enough. Just tell them to come
19   by the class after school. I'll be in my room at that
20   time and I can take over.
21 MADDIE: Oh, all right. That will work.
22 MRS. STONE: Good. Maddie, I need to run some papers to
23   the office. Do you mind waiting around here while I
24   do that? I usually have a handful of students who
25   come in early before the bell rings.
26 MADDIE: No, I don't mind at all.
27 MRS. STONE: Great. I'll be back shortly. *(Exits.)*
28 MADDIE: *(Goes to the MRS. STONE's desk and stands*
29   *behind it. Looks around as she thinks about being the*
30   *teacher.)* I'm Miss Cole, your teacher. That's right.
31   Your third period teacher. And what I say goes. It's my
32   rules or the highway. Make that the principal's office.
33   So, don't give me any of your nonsense. Do you hear?
34   *(Slams hand on desk.)* Do you hear?!
35 GARRETT: *(Enters.)* Where's Mrs. Stone?

1   MADDIE: *(Sits at the desk.)* **Not here.**

2   **GARRETT: Are you the sub?**

3   **MADDIE: For now.**

4   **GARRETT: What are we doing today?**

5   **MADDIE: I imagine we'll do whatever it is I tell you to do.**

6   **Don't you think?**

7   **GARRETT: Whoa! A mean sub.** *(Sits down.)* **Mrs. Stone is**

8   **an easy teacher. She only gives us word searches and**

9   **crossword puzzles in here. Her class is fun.**

10   **MADDIE: Well, she's not here today, is she?**

11   **GARRETT: No ma'am.** *(Stands.)* **Uh ... maybe I'll just wait**

12   **outside in the hall until the bell rings. I usually like**

13   **to come in here early and chat with Mrs. Stone, but**

14   **since she's not here ...** *(Starts toward the door.)*

15   **MADDIE: Sit down! The bell's about to ring. No use**

16   **wandering the halls.**

17   **GARRETT:** *(Sits down.)* **Yes ma'am.**

18   **JOSH:** *(Enters.)* **Hey. Where's Mrs. Stone?**

19   **MADDIE: Obviously not here.**

20   **JOSH: Oh, sub today.**

21   **MADDIE: My name is not sub today, it's Miss Cole. You**

22   **may call me that. Miss Cole.**

23   **JOSH: When's Mrs. Stone coming back?**

24   **MADDIE: That's for me to know and you to find out.**

25   **JOSH: Dang! You're a mean sub.**

26   **MADDIE: It's Miss Cole and you haven't seen mean yet.**

27   **JOSH: I think I'll wait outside in the hall.**

28   **MADDIE: Sit down!**

29   **JOSH: But ...**

30   **MADDIE: Sit.** *(JOSH sits down. MADDIE stands.)* **Let's**

31   **begin.**

32   **GARRETT: Aren't you going to wait until the bell rings?**

33   **The other students aren't even in here yet.**

34   **MADDIE: Don't tell me how to teach.**

35   **JOSH: But the bell hasn't even rung.**

1 **MADDIE: Let's begin. Open your textbooks to page one-**
2   **twenty-three.** *(Points to GARRETT.)* **You, read the first**
3   **paragraph.**
4 **GARRETT:** *(Opens book.)* **"In 1812, the United States**
5   **declared war against Great Britain."**
6 **HAILEY:** *(Enters.)* **Class already started? I didn't even hear**
7   **the bell.**
8 **MADDIE: Class has started. Sit down.**
9 **HAILEY:** *(Sits down, looks around.)* **Where is everyone else?**
10   *(Jumps up.)* **Did I miss the rapture?**
11 **MADDIE: Sit down! Open your book to page one-twenty-**
12   **three.** *(Slams hand on desk.)* **Now.**
13 **HAILEY:** *(Opens book.)* **I think I did miss it.**
14 **MADDIE:** *(Points at GARRETT.)* **You! Continue reading.**
15 **GARRETT: "In 1812, the United States declared war**
16   **against Great Britain. For the previous twenty years,**
17   **Britain had claimed the right to intercept American**
18   **ships on the high seas — "**
19 **HAILEY: Excuse me, but Mrs. Stone never makes us read.**
20   **She gives us word searches and crossword puzzles.**
21 **MADDIE: And I'm not Mrs. Stone, am I?**
22 **HAILEY: No ma'am.**
23 **MADDIE:** *(Claps her hands together.)* **Let's have a pop quiz!**
24 **JOSH: Over what?**
25 **GARRETT: Mrs. Stone never gave us pop quizzes.**
26 **MADDIE: Question number one.** *(The students quickly*
27   *grab paper and pens.)* **What were the causes of the War**
28   **of 1812?**
29 **HAILEY:** *(Under her breath, to the others)* **I don't know this.**
30 **JOSH: I don't either.**
31 **MADDIE: Question number two. When was the War of**
32   **1812?**
33 **GARRETT:** *(Under his breath to the others. Writing)* **I'm**
34   **putting 1812.**
35 **HAILEY: Me too.**

1   JOSH: Makes logical sense to me. *(Writes.)* **1812. Surely I**
2   **got this one right.**
3   MADDIE: Question number three. **What weapons were**
4   **used in the War of 1812?**
5   JOSH: I'm guessing helicopters and Stealth Fighters and
6   **M14 Rifles.**
7   GARRETT: I'm going with your answers.
8   HAILEY: Sounds good to me.
9   MADDIE: Question number four. **What was the**
10   **significance of the War of 1812?**
11   GARRETT: Heck if I know.
12   HAILEY: I'm not even sure what that question means.
13   JOSH: Where are our word searches? I miss them.
14   MADDIE: Quiet please! **Turn in your papers now.**
15   *(GARRETT, JOSH, and HAILEY take their papers to*
16   *MADDIE. She gets out a red pen and begins to grade*
17   *them.)* **Zero. Zero. And Zero.**
18   GARRETT: Ouch!
19   MADDIE: That will look great in the grade book, don't you
20   **think?**
21   JOSH: But Miss Cole, the bell hasn't even rung yet.
22   HAILEY: It didn't? I didn't miss the rapture after all?
23   GARRETT: I'm never coming to class early again.
24   JOSH: Me neither.
25   MADDIE: *(Opens grade book.)* **Let me just enter these**
26   **zeros in the grade book with my red pen.**
27   MRS. STONE: *(Enters.)* **I'm back!** *(The students rush to*
28   *MRS. STONE and begin hugging her.)*
29   GARRETT: Mrs. Stone, you're back.
30   JOSH: We missed you.
31   HAILEY: Please never leave us again.
32   JOSH: We love you.
33   MRS. STONE: Oh, my goodness. What a welcome! And I
34   love all you, too. *(Turns to MADDIE.)* **How'd it go?**
35   MADDIE: *(Smiles.)* **Great! I can't wait till third period.**

30. Tornado Drill

CAST: (2M, 2F) ABBY, LEXI, LUIS, BROCK
PROPS: Two cell phones
SETTING: School hallway

1   *(At rise, ABBY and LEXI are sitting on the floor, against*
2   *the wall.)*
3   **ABBY:** Do you think this is a drill or a real tornado is coming
4   our way?
5   **LEXI:** I don't know. It's cloudy outside. And earlier I thought
6   I heard thunder.
7   **ABBY:** So did I. Which means it's the real thing.
8   **LEXI:** You know, I've sometimes wished the school would
9   blow away, but I didn't want to be inside of it when it
10   happened.
11   **ABBY:** Are you scared?
12   **LEXI:** Yes. And I'm starting to have regrets, too.
13   **ABBY:** About your life?
14   **LEXI:** Yes. Unfinished business. *(Yells down the hall.)* Luis,
15   I'm sorry. I still love you.
16   **ABBY:** What are you doing? You still love Luis?
17   **LEXI:** I hope he heard me.
18   **ABBY:** I'm sure he did. I have some regrets too. Realizing
19   how short life really is. It's too short to be miserable.
20   *(Yells down the hall.)* Aaron, it's over. Me and you ...
21   we're finished.
22   **LEXI:** We may all be finished.
23   **ABBY:** I think he heard me. I'm just tired of Aaron. And if we
24   come out of this alive, I'm letting Brock know how I
25   really feel about him.
26   **LEXI:** But we might not come out of this alive.
27   **ABBY:** Do you see Brock anywhere?
28   **LEXI:** *(Looks, then points.)* Against the wall next to Jade.
29   **ABBY:** *(Yells out.)* Brock, I love you. I've loved you since the
30   sixth grade.

1   LEXI: Brock is giving you a strange look.

2   ABBY: Well, at least he knows the truth now. Oh, I just
3   thought of something else I want to get off my chest.
4   *(Yells.)* Mr. Morris, it was me. I'm the one who stole
5   the Snickers candy bar off your desk. I'm sorry. You
6   punished the whole class for it, but it was me. I did it.
7   And I'm sorry. If I come out of this alive, I'll buy you
8   a new Snickers bar.

9   LEXI: Why did you eat Mr. Morris' Snickers bar?

10   ABBY: I was hungry.

11   LEXI: Yeah ... confession time. *(Takes out her cell phone.)* I
12   need to text my mom. "Oh, Mom ... I lied."

13   ABBY: I need to do that. *(Takes out her cell phone.)* "Mom,
14   I lied."

15   LEXI: We're both bad.

16   ABBY: I know. But nothing like being close to death to
17   turn a person around.

18   LEXI: *(Texts.)* "Mom, I didn't go to the skate park with
19   Chrissy."

20   ABBY: *(Texts.)* "I didn't go to the mall with Alicia."

21   LEXI: *(Texts.)* "I met Nate."

22   ABBY: *(Texts.)* "I met Tim."

23   LEXI: *(Texts.)* "Mom, I know it was wrong!"

24   ABBY: *(Texts.)* "I know it was wrong!"

25   LEXI: *(Texts.)* "And I broke up with Nate. You never liked
26   him."

27   ABBY: *(Texts.)* "Mom, I don't like Tim. He was a bad
28   influence on me."

29   LEXI: *(Texts.)* "And there's more."

30   ABBY: *(Texts.)* "So much more."

31   LEXI: *(Texts.)* "I didn't write Grandma that thank you note."

32   ABBY: *(Texts.)* "I'm the one who lost your earrings."

33   LEXI: *(Texts.)* "I didn't stay after school for help with
34   homework."

35   ABBY: I'm guilty of that one, too. *(Texts.)* "I didn't stay
36   after school for help with homework."

1   **LEXI:** *(Texts.)* "I stayed to make out with Nate. But Mom, I
2   dumped him."
3   **ABBY:** *(Texts.)* "I stayed to flirt with Brock."
4   **LEXI:** And how did that go?
5   **ABBY:** Great. Brock always hangs around the parking lot
6   after school. So I stayed around too. We talked, joked
7   around, laughed ... And all of a sudden it hit me. I
8   loved him!
9   **LEXI:** Wow.
10   **ABBY:** I do. *(Yells.)* Brock, I love you. I always have. I always
11   will.
12   **LEXI:** *(Looking down the hall)* He's covering his head.
13   **ABBY:** Because we're supposed to, Lexi.
14   **LEXI:** Or he's embarrassed.
15   **ABBY:** I'm the one who should be embarrassed. But we're
16   about to blow away, so why do I care?
17   **LEXI:** *(Texts.)* "And mom ... I snuck out of the house ...
18   twice. It was Nate's idea. And Mom, I broke up with
19   Nate."
20   **ABBY:** *(Texts.)* "Mom ... I paid Timmy to do my chores. He
21   needed the money and I'm lazy. That's why I never
22   have any money, Mom. And Timmy's rich ... thanks to
23   me."
24   **LEXI:** *(Texts.)* "I'm a liar."
25   **ABBY:** Me too! *(Texts.)* "I'm a liar."
26   **LEXI:** *(Texts.)* "Pretended to be sick."
27   **ABBY:** Me too! *(Texts.)* "Pretended to be sick."
28   **LEXI:** *(Texts.)* "Cheated."
29   **ABBY:** *(Texts.)* "Snuck around."
30   **LEXI:** *(Texts.)* "Told half-truths."
31   **ABBY:** *(Texts.)* "Forged your signature."
32   **LEXI:** *(Texts.)* "Changed grades."
33   **ABBY:** *(Texts.)* "Wrote bad things about you in my diary.
34   But the bottom line is ... I love you Mom."
35   **LEXI:** "I love you Mom!" *(Yells.)* I still love you, Luis. Give us
36   another chance.

1 ABBY: *(Yells.)* Brock, my heart is yours. And I want to tell
2   the world. I love you!
3 LEXI: I think you did just tell the world.
4 LUIS: *(Runs over and sits next to LEXI.)* You want me to give
5   us another chance?
6 LEXI: Luis, how'd you get over here?
7 LUIS: When Coach Jenkins wasn't looking I ran for it.
8 LEXI: Oh, Luis! If we make it through this, let's start over.
9   Let's forget the past. Forget about hurtful words.
10   Let's make a fresh start.
11 LUIS: You mean that?
12 LEXI: Yes! And I wish we weren't about to die in this
13   tornado because that's exactly what I want.
14 LUIS: We're not about to die. It's just a drill.
15 LEXI: How do you know?
16 LUIS: I heard Coach Jenkins telling Mrs. Phillips that it
17   was just a drill. They did it on a stormy day so the
18   students would take the drill seriously.
19 ABBY: You mean it's just a drill?
20 LUIS: Yes. And this is great, Lexi. I'm so glad we're getting
21   back together.
22 ABBY: Luis, are you a hundred percent sure it's only a
23   drill?
24 LUIS: I am. I heard the teachers talking about it.
25 ABBY: Great. And I've been yelling to Brock and for the
26   entire world to hear that I love him.
27 LUIS: I even texted my mom earlier and she assured me
28   that there were no tornadoes around.
29 LEXI: And I confessed every sin to my mom by text.
30 ABBY: Me too.
31 LEXI: Great. We are going to be so grounded.
32 ABBY: Now I wish the tornado would hit us.
33 LEXI: I'm with you.
34 LUIS: *(To LEXI)* I want to do this right. Lexi, will you go out
35   with me?

1   LEXI: Before I answer that question I want to ask you a
2   question. What about Maria?
3   LUIS: Maria and I are still friends.
4   LEXI: Are you still kissing your friend Maria?
5   LUIS: Let's leave the past in the past. All right, Lexi?
6   LEXI: Luis, how many times have you kissed Maria?
7   LUIS: How many?
8   ABBY: You know, I just want the tornado to blow me away
9   right now. How could I have yelled to Brock that I love
10   him? *(Arms in air)* Take me now. Please take me now!
11   LEXI: How many times, Luis?
12   LUIS: *(Thinking)* Uh ... forty or fifty times. But you broke
13   up with me, Lexi. Remember? And before that it was
14   only about a dozen times.
15   LEXI: No!
16   LUIS: No?
17   LEXI: No, I don't want to go out with you.
18   LUIS: But you just said you still loved me.
19   LEXI: I thought I was going to die, Luis.
20   ABBY: I thought I was going to die too. And now I want to
21   disappear. Now that Brock knows I love him. *(Arms in*
22   *air)* Please, just take me now!
23   LUIS: We're not getting back together?
24   LEXI: No!
25   LUIS: Fine! *(Exits.)*
26   LEXI: Glad that is settled once and for all.
27   BROCK: *(Runs over and sits next to ABBY.)* Why do you keep
28   yelling that you love me?
29   ABBY: Brock!
30   LEXI: *(To BROCK)* It was a dare. Now Abby's in the club.
31   Yea!
32   BROCK: Oh, OK. Because my girlfriend is pretty hacked.
33   But I'll go back and tell her it was a dare for club
34   membership. What's the name of the club?
35   ABBY: The uh ... uh ...

1   **LEXI: The Girls Club.**

2   **BROCK: The Girls Club?**

3   **LEXI: That's right.**

4   **ABBY: Sorry if I embarrassed you.**

5   **BROCK: It's OK. I once had to ask a girl to marry me. For**

6   **a dare.** *(Laughs.)* **I'm glad she said no!**

7   **ABBY: I bet.**

8   **BROCK: OK, see you later. And I'll tell my girlfriend**

9   **everything is OK. You don't love me. Which is good**

10   **because I don't love you either.** *(Exits.)*

11   **ABBY: I hate my life.**

12   **LEXI: I never want to go home again.**

13   **ABBY: Home. Oh, Mom!** *(Texts.)* **"Mom, I love you more**

14   **than anything!"**

15   **LEXI:** *(Texts.)* **"Mom, I almost died today!"**

16   **ABBY:** *(Texts.)* **"Which makes me realize the important**

17   **things in life."**

18   **LEXI:** *(Texts.)* **"Truth."**

19   **ABBY:** *(Texts.)* **"Honesty."**

20   **LEXI:** *(Texts.)* **"Responsibility."**

21   **ABBY:** *(Texts.)* **"Hard work."**

22   **LEXI:** *(Texts.)* **"Respect."**

23   **ABBY:** *(Texts.)* **"Following rules."**

24   **LEXI:** *(Texts.)* **"And love."**

25   **ABBY:** *(Texts.)* **"Love. The greatest gift of all!"**

26   **LEXI:** *(Texts.)* **"Mom, please forgive me!"**

27   **ABBY:** *(Texts.)* **"I'm sorry, Mom! Forgive me!"**

28   **LEXI:** *(Texts.)* **"I almost died!"**

29   **ABBY:** *(Texts.)* **"I almost died."**

30   **LEXI:** *(To ABBY)* **We are going to be in so much trouble**

31   **when we get home.**

32   **ABBY: I'll never see the light of day again.**

33   **LEXI and ABBY:** *(Arms heavenward)* **Please, just take me**

34   **away now!**

35

31. 15 1/2

CAST: (1M, 2F) LILLIAN, JADE, CHRIS
PROPS: Two sets of car keys
SETTING: Outside school

1   **LILLIAN: I'm fifteen ... and a half.**

2   **JADE: Sixteen. Driver's license!**

3   **CHRIS: Sixteen here. Driving and dating!**

4   **LILLIAN: I get to drive ... with an adult. But dating ... not**
5   **until I'm sixteen.**

6   **JADE: Sixteen and never been kissed.**

7   **CHRIS:** *(Looks at JADE.)* **Really?** *(JADE smiles and nods at*
8   *CHRIS.)*

9   **LILLIAN: Fifteen ... and a half. Does anything exciting**
10   **happen at fifteen?**

11   **JADE: Oh, and I start work tomorrow at Corn Dogs & Fries.**
12   **"May I take your order?"**

13   **CHRIS: Well, I have to work. Not only do I need gas money,**
14   **but date money as well.**

15   **LILLIAN: I tried to get a job. "I'm sorry, sweetheart. But we**
16   **only hire sixteen year olds. Why don't you come back in**
17   **a few months?"**

18   **JADE: Don't you just hate being fifteen?**

19   **CHRIS: I hated it.**

20   **LILLIAN: I'm beginning to.**

21   **JADE: It's like the whole world is passing you by.**

22   **CHRIS:** *(Rattling his keys)* **Hello, world!**

23   **JADE: Don't you just love having a driver's license?**

24   **CHRIS: I'm free.**

25   **JADE: Hello world, here I come.**

26   **LILLIAN: I need a ride.**

27   **JADE: I'll give you a ride. Where do you need to go?**

28   **LILLIAN: Home, I guess.**

29   **CHRIS: Gone are the days of walking home. "Hey, look at**

1 me, you little people out there walking down the
2 street. I'm driving now!"
3 JADE: Dad put my bike in the shed. *(Rattles her keys.)* I
4 never ride it anymore.
5 LILLIAN: I ride my bike to school.
6 JADE: At least you're getting exercise.
7 CHRIS: Positive thinking. I like positive thinking. But
8 most of all ... I love being sixteen!
9 JADE: Me too. Sixteen ... and never been kissed.
10 CHRIS: Really?
11 JADE: Really.
12 LILLIAN: I'm fifteen ... and a half ... and never been kissed.
13 But that doesn't sound very tragic or romantic, does
14 it?
15 CHRIS: I'd hate to be fifteen.
16 JADE: Me too.
17 CHRIS: Those awkward years.
18 JADE: "How old are you, dear?" Fifteen. "Well, bless your
19 heart."
20 CHRIS: The liberating age of sixteen.
21 JADE: Freedom!
22 CHRIS: And two years away from becoming an adult.
23 JADE: Respect.
24 CHRIS: Responsibility.
25 JADE: College.
26 CHRIS: Parties!
27 JADE: Curfew? Ha!
28 CHRIS: Asking permission? Ha!
29 JADE: Freedom!
30 LILLIAN: I wish I were eighteen. Or even sixteen.
31 JADE: *(Tosses keys.)* Yes, it's great to be sixteen.
32 CHRIS: *(Tosses keys.)* Driving, dating ...
33 LILLIAN: I took driver's ed.
34 CHRIS: I remember those days.
35 JADE: Me too. I was all enthusiastic about learning how to

1   **drive.** *(Tosses keys.)* **Now it feels like I've been driving**

2   **forever.**

3 **CHRIS: Yes. I almost can't remember *not* driving.**

4 **LILLIAN: At least I have my driver's permit.**

5 **CHRIS: Hey, if I see you coming, I'll pull over to the side.**

6   *(Laughs.)*

7 **JADE: Yes, you inexperienced drivers can be very scary out**

8   **there.**

9 **CHRIS: Look out! Here she comes. Get outta her way!**

10 **JADE: The first time my dad let me back out of the garage**

11   **was a nightmare. Instead of putting the car in**

12   **reverse, I put it in drive. My dad was screaming at me.**

13   **"Brake it! Brake it!" But I couldn't seem to remember**

14   **which was the gas pedal and which was the brake.**

15   **Needless to say, I plowed right into the wall. Huge**

16   **hole in the garage wall. My brother said, "Cool! You**

17   **can see right into the den from the garage now." Dad**

18   **was not happy.**

19 **CHRIS: And I ran over my sister's bike. Forgot to look back**

20   **before backing up. Crushed that sucker into a million**

21   **pieces.**

22 **LILLIAN: I haven't hit anything yet.**

23 **CHRIS: Give it time. Give it time. You will.**

24 **JADE: But hopefully it won't be another car.**

25 **CHRIS:** *(Makes screeching sounds, then crashing sounds.)*

26   **Oops!**

27 **LILLIAN: I wouldn't do that.**

28 **JADE: Don't you remember the statistics from driver's ed?**

29   **Statistics are, teen drivers are ten times more likely to**

30   **be involved in an automobile crash.**

31 **CHRIS: Higher statistics if you add running over bikes,**

32   **crashing into the garage walls, and tearing side**

33   **mirrors off in the drive-thru lane.**

34 **JADE: Did you do that?**

35 **CHRIS: Hey, I'm not admitting to anything.**

1   JADE: Well, I ran over plenty of curbs.

2   CHRIS: Did that.

3   JADE: I almost hit a puppy.

4   LILLIAN: Oh no!

5   JADE: But I didn't.

6   CHRIS: I backed into a dumpster.

7   JADE: I did that, too.

8   CHRIS: And I once drove the wrong way on a one-way
9   street.

10   JADE: That's dangerous.

11   CHRIS: I know! Believe me. When I saw what I was doing,
12   I turned the corner and realized I could have crashed
13   big time.

14   JADE: I turned on my wiper blades and couldn't figure out
15   how to turn them off. I looked like a dummy driving
16   around the school parking lot. Loser!

17   CHRIS: *(Tosses keys.)* But those inexperienced days are
18   over for me. I'm a pro.

19   JADE: Me too.

20   LILLIAN: I can't wait to drive without adult supervision.

21   CHRIS: Have to wait till you're sixteen.

22   LILLIAN: I know. I'm fifteen ... and a half. Six more
23   months.

24   JADE: I'm sixteen ... and never been kissed.

25   CHRIS: Really?

26   JADE: Really. *(They share a smile.)*

27   CHRIS: *(Tosses keys.)* Well, off to work I go. See you guys
28   later. Oh, and Jade, maybe we should catch a movie
29   sometime.

30   JADE: That'd be great. Bye.

31   LILLIAN: Bye.

32   CHRIS: Bye. *(Exits.)*

33   JADE: *(To LILLIAN)* You need a ride?

34   LILLIAN: I do.

35   JADE: Come on. I'll take you.

1   **LILLIAN: Thanks.**
2   **JADE:** *(Tosses keys.)* **Let's go. I haven't driven off a curb or**
3   **run into anything big in at least a week, so don't be**
4   **nervous. I'm really a safe driver. Except when I get**
5   **distracted. Like when Tiffany was screaming and**
6   **telling me to look at these guys running track, I**
7   **plowed right over a water sprinkler. But that was a**
8   **week ago. And it didn't do any damage to my car.**
9   **Thank goodness! I love driving. I love being sixteen.**
10   **Don't you just hate being fifteen?**
11   **LILLIAN: Yes. Fifteen ... and a half.** *(They exit.)*

32. The Chicken Dance

CAST: (1M, 3F) CHAD, JULIE, ALICIA, MRS. RIGGS
SETTING: Outside the principal's office

1   *(At rise, CHAD enters and sits next to JULIE and ALICIA.)*
2   **CHAD:** Man, I hate being sent to the principal's office. Is Mr.
3   Hogan here?
4   **JULIE:** Yes. He has another student in his office.
5   **ALICIA:** And he was screaming at that person a minute ago.
6   **CHAD:** Oh boy. Can't wait for that.
7   **JULIE:** You're after us.
8   **CHAD:** Right. If you girls could just get him in a good mood
9   before I go in there, that'd be great.
10 **ALICIA:** I doubt that. Mr. Hogan is all about rules and
11   following them.
12 **JULIE:** I don't think I've ever seen him crack a smile.
13 **ALICIA:** Me neither. And I hope he'll let us go in together. I
14   don't like that one-on-one thing.
15 **CHAD:** What are you two in here for?
16 **JULIE:** Fighting.
17 **CHAD:** With each other?
18 **ALICIA:** Yes.
19 **CHAD:** Over what? Wait. Let me guess. You were fighting
20   over a boy.
21 **JULIE:** Good guess. And you're right.
22 **CHAD:** You girls. Always fighting over boys. Why is that? And
23   why don't you girls ever fight over me? Hey, since
24   you're already in trouble for fighting over some dude,
25   how about fighting over me? I want to see what if feels
26   like. Please!
27 **ALICIA:** We're through fighting over boys.
28 **JULIE:** Yes. We realized they are just not worth the effort.
29 **CHAD:** Ah, come on. Fight over me. Please.
30 **ALICIA:** *(To JULIE)* Why did we even waste our time fighting

1   over **Bobby?** *(To CHAD)* **Julie and I found out that**
2   **Bobby was playing both of us.**
3 **JULIE: I was his one and only.**
4 **ALICIA: No, I was his one and only.**
5 **JULIE: And it wasn't his fault other girls like you flirted**
6   **with him.**
7 **ALICIA: I was just being too sensitive. Julie had a thing for**
8   **him, but he didn't care one iota for you.**
9 **JULIE: And he wouldn't give Alicia the time of day. But he**
10   **did.**
11 **ALICIA: And you too.**
12 **JULIE: Thought he could keep his two-timing ways a**
13   **secret.**
14 **ALICIA: Well, today it all came crashing down on Bobby.**
15 **JULIE: After of course Alicia and I had a scuffle in the**
16   **hallway.**
17 **ALICIA: "Keep your hands off *my* boyfriend."**
18 **JULIE: "What do you mean? That's *my* boyfriend!"**
19 **ALICIA: "Someone here is having hallucinations!"**
20 **JULIE: "And that someone would be you!"**
21 **ALICIA: "No you!"**
22 **JULIE: "No you!"**
23 **MRS. RIGGS:** *(Enters, hands on hips.)* **What is going on**
24   **here? Are you two girls fighting again?**
25 **ALICIA: No, we were just ...**
26 **MRS. RIGGS: Just can't let it go, can you?**
27 **JULIE: No, we did, we were just —**
28 **MRS. RIGGS:** *(Points to CHAD.)* **You!**
29 **CHAD: Me? What did I do?**
30 **MRS. RIGGS: You sit between those two girls.**
31 **CHAD:** *(Smiles.)* **OK. I don't mind doing that.**
32 **MRS. RIGGS: You'd think you two girls could let it go.**
33   **Especially before going in to see Mr. Hogan. He is not**
34   **going to be happy about this. When I tell him you**
35   **were still fighting outside his office ... Well, it will**

1   probably send him over the edge. Student after
2   student has been in here today. Misbehaving,
3   fighting ... *(Looks at CHAD.)* Acting like an idiot. So I
4   just say whatever Mr. Hogan hands out to you ... you
5   deserve. So, get ready. Now sit here and be quiet.
6   *(Exits.)*
7 ALICIA: Oh my gosh! Mrs. Riggs is as mean as Mr. Hogan.
8 JULIE: I guess she'd have to be seeing that she's Mr.
9   Hogan's secretary.
10 CHAD: This is not looking good for us, girls. Wish we
11   could just sneak on out of here.
12 JULIE: We can't. And even if we tried, we'd never get past
13   Mrs. Riggs.
14 ALICIA: So, Chad, you haven't told us. What are you in
15   here for?
16 CHAD: Let's not go there.
17 JULIE: That's not fair. We told you what we did.
18 CHAD: I was just acting stupid.
19 ALICIA: Acting like an idiot is what Mrs. Riggs called it. So
20   what did you do?
21 JULIE: Tell us.
22 CHAD: All right, all right, I'll tell you. I did my chicken
23   dance in math class when Mr. Solis left the room.
24 JULIE: The *what* dance?
25 ALICIA: The chicken dance?
26 CHAD: Yeah. I have this chicken dance thing that I do. My
27   friends have seen it and they love it. So when Mr.
28   Solis left the room during math class, the guys were
29   like, "Come on, Chad. Do it! Do it! Do your chicken
30   dance for us!" I'd blame my actions on peer pressure,
31   but I have a feeling Mr. Hogan is not going to be
32   receptive to that idea. The guys kept on. "Chicken
33   dance! Chicken dance! Chicken dance!"
34 ALICIA: What the heck is a chicken dance?
35 CHAD: It's just something I do. It's funny. And let me tell

1   you, I had the entire class rolling on the floor. Have to
2   admit I liked the attention. I was at the front of the
3   classroom doing my chicken dance, the class loving
4   it, laughing till they cried, and in walks Mr. Solis. Of
5   course everyone sees Mr. Solis except for me. I
6   wondered why they quit laughing. But I just kept on
7   going. Continued with my chicken dance and not
8   seeing Mr. Solis until I plowed right into him. He
9   didn't say a thing. Wrote me a pass and here I am.

10 JULIE: I want to see your chicken dance.

11 CHAD: Oh no.

12 ALICIA: Me too. I bet it's funny!

13 CHAD: Mr. Solis didn't think so. He was so mad he didn't
14   even say a word. No wait, he did say one word. After
15   he wrote me the pass to the principal's office, he said,
16   "Out."

17 JULIE: I'm thinking detention for you.

18 ALICIA: What about us? We're going to get it, too.

19 JULIE: Unless we can be smart about this. Go in and cry
20   and put all the blame on Bobby for lying to us.

21 ALICIA: We can try.

22 CHAD: Won't work.

23 ALICIA: Well, nothing you can do is getting you off from
24   doing the chicken dance in math class.

25 CHAD: Unless I can find a good excuse.

26 JULIE: An excuse for the chicken dance?

27 CHAD: Ants in my pants?

28 ALICIA: No way.

29 CHAD: Cramp in my leg?

30 JULIE: Mr. Hogan won't fall for it.

31 CHAD: Exercising for brainpower?

32 ALICIA: Face it, Chad, you're looking at detention. Just like
33   Julie and I.

34 CHAD: I know. But I have to try. "Mr. Hogan, math is hard
35   for me. And to unlock extra brain resources, it helps

1   when I move around."
2 JULIE: Like a chicken?
3 ALICIA: In front of the entire class?
4 CHAD: "It was a poor decision, Mr. Hogan. One I will
5   never repeat again."
6 JULIE: "Don't give me your lame excuses, you chicken
7   dancer you! You are going to detention. And there
8   you may have all the time you need to unlock those
9   extra brain resources!"
10 CHAD: Detention for a chicken dance. How stupid is that?
11 ALICIA: Don't say that to Mr. Hogan.
12 CHAD: I'm not, but I can think it.
13 JULIE: So do it for us.
14 CHAD: No.
15 ALICIA: Yeah! I want to see this chicken dance of yours.
16 CHAD: No. My chicken dancing days are over.
17 JULIE: One more time. Please.
18 ALICIA: Come on, Chad. Please!
19 CHAD: Nope. Not going to.
20 JULIE: *(Touches his arm.)* Please. For me.
21 ALICIA: *(Touches his other arm.)* Please. For me.
22 CHAD: Oh, all right. *(Stands.)* But this is the last time. *(He*
23   *begins his chicken dance, flopping his arms, taking*
24   *high steps, and bobbing his head back and forth.)*
25   "Bawk, bawk, bawk, bawk bawk! Bawk, bawk, bawk,
26   bawk bawk!"
27 JULIE and ALICIA: *(Laughing)* That's great! I love it! *(CHAD*
28   *continues with the dance. MRS. RIGGS enters, staring*
29   *at him. CHAD turns around and sees her, then stops.)*
30 MRS. RIGGS: Now that was funny. My granddaughter
31   would love that! Do it again.
32 CHAD: What? No. No I can't.
33 MRS. RIGGS: No, it's great. I love it! *(To the GIRLS)* Is he
34   too funny or what?
35 CHAD: But Mrs. Riggs, I got into trouble for this.

1 **MRS. RIGGS: For that? But that is totally hilarious. That's**
2   **the funniest thing I've ever seen.**
3 **CHAD: But ...**
4 **MRS. RIGGS: I need to laugh more often. The stress in this**
5   **office just wears me down.** *(Laughs.)* **But that was**
6   **great. Do it again.**
7 **CHAD: But Mrs. Riggs, I don't want to get into any more**
8   **trouble.**
9 **MRS. RIGGS: I tell you what. If you do the chicken dance**
10   **for me one more time, I'll let you go back to your**
11   **class.**
12 **CHAD: Without seeing Mr. Hogan?**
13 **MRS. RIGGS: Without seeing Mr. Hogan.** *(Laughing)* **Come**
14   **on! Do it again.**
15 **CHAD: Well, all right.** *(Does the chicken dance as the others*
16   *laugh. To MRS. RIGGS after he has finished)* **Can I go**
17   **now?**
18 **MRS. RIGGS:** *(Laughing)* **Go, go! You're forgiven.** *(CHAD*
19   *exits.)* **That was just the funniest thing I ever saw. I**
20   **wonder ... I just wonder if I could do the chicken**
21   **dance? Maybe ...** *(Attempts to do the chicken dance as*
22   *she exits.)*

33. First Kiss

CAST: (2M, 2F) REAGAN, ALEXIS, JAKE, BOBBY
SETTING: Outside of school

1 REAGAN: Here's the plan. Jake and I are going to sneak into
2   the choir room during lunch.
3 ALEXIS: What if Mrs. Lange sees you?
4 REAGAN: She won't. She always turns off the lights and
5   leaves for lunch. We might even go into one of the
6   practice rooms just in case.
7 ALEXIS: Just in case Mrs. Lange comes back early from
8   lunch? So she doesn't interrupt your first kiss! Are you
9   scared?
10 REAGAN: I'm more scared of never being kissed.
11 ALEXIS: So are you going to close your eyes or keep them
12   open so you can watch?
13 REAGAN: I don't know. What are you supposed to do?
14 ALEXIS: Well as an expert, I can tell you that it's best to close
15   your eyes. Because if you don't and Jake doesn't either,
16   it can be awkward to be staring at each other so closely.
17 REAGAN: Then I'll close my eyes. So Alexis, when was your
18   first kiss?
19 ALEXIS: Not counting cousins and a boy in sixth grade ... last
20   year.
21 REAGAN: Who with?
22 ALEXIS: Ricky. And it almost didn't happen. We'd talked
23   about it. Planned on it. I was waiting for it. But Ricky
24   and I sat in the back row of the theatre staring at the
25   movie screen. His hand was in the buttered popcorn
26   most of the time. I couldn't eat. I was nervous. But I
27   was thinking, "Do it, already."
28 REAGAN: And?
29 ALEXIS: And I moved my shoulder closer to his. But he just
30   grabbed the popcorn bucket and shifted his weight to

1   the other side of the chair. I was thinking, "Really?"

2 REGAN: Then what?

3 ALEXIS: Then I tried putting my head on his shoulder, but

4   he started squirming in his chair as if it bothered

5   him.

6 REAGAN: Ricky must have been nervous.

7 ALEXIS: Well, I was getting frustrated. We'd been going

8   together for a whole month and he'd yet to kiss me.

9 REAGAN: And did he?

10 ALEXIS: After I turned to him and said, "Are you going to

11   kiss me or what?" He shrugged. I grabbed the bucket

12   of popcorn, dumped it in his lap, then said I was

13   leaving. Then he grabbed my arm and kissed me on

14   the cheek. Finally.

15 REAGAN: The cheek?

16 ALEXIS: It was a kiss. Maybe not on the lips ...

17 REAGAN: But a boy has kissed you on the lips, right?

18 ALEXIS: Does my three-year-old nephew count?

19 REAGAN: No! Alexis, I thought you were the expert at this

20   kissing thing.

21 ALEXIS: Reagan, I'm saving my lips for the right guy. Are

22   you sure Jake is the right guy?

23 REAGAN: Yes. I want him to kiss me. I want to experience

24   my first kiss with him.

25 ALEXIS: You could practice on your hand. Like this. *(Kisses*

26   *her hand.)*

27 REAGAN: Everyone's done that. But I don't think that

28   really prepares you for the real thing.

29 ALEXIS: Has Jake kissed many girls?

30 REAGAN: Three. Melissa, Callie, and Breanna.

31 ALEXIS: Really?

32 REAGAN: They were on a choir trip and he kissed them on

33   the bus.

34 ALEXIS: Oh. Does Jake know this will be your first kiss?

35 REAGAN: No. I told him I'd kissed several boys.

1   ALEXIS: Why?

2   REAGAN: I didn't want to sound all inexperienced.

3   ALEXIS: I don't blame you there. Oh, look! Here he comes.

4   REAGAN: Who?

5   ALEXIS: Jake! He's heading this way with Bobby.

6   REAGAN: Oh, wow. OK. I'm starting to feel nervous now.

7   ALEXIS: Just act normal. And let's pretend we were

8   talking about something besides Jake kissing you.

9   Like ... uh ... uh ... Veronica's pierced eyebrow. So ... do

10   you like it?

11 REAGAN: *(Not listening)* What?

12 ALEXIS: Veronica's eyebrow.

13 REAGAN: What about Veronica's eyebrow?

14 ALEXIS: She pierced it.

15 REAGAN: She did?

16 ALEXIS: Do you like it?

17 REAGAN: Like what? *(JAKE and BOBBY enter.)*

18 JAKE: Hey.

19 REAGAN: Hey.

20 ALEXIS: Hey, Jake. Lunch plans?

21 JAKE: What?

22 REAGAN: Alexis just asked me to grab lunch with her at

23   the snack bar.

24 ALEXIS: Do you want to come too?

25 JAKE: Sorry, I can't.

26 ALEXIS: Oh, why not?

27 JAKE: I, uh ...

28 BOBBY: He needs to go to the choir room.

29 REAGAN: *(To JAKE)* You told him?

30 BOBBY: Of course he told me. We're best buds.

31 ALEXIS: She told me too. And isn't this exciting. First kiss!

32 REAGAN: Alexis!

33 ALEXIS: I mean, first kiss between you two.

34 BOBBY: But I wonder if planning it out ruins the

35   romance?

1 ALEXIS: Do you think?

2 BOBBY: I'm more of a spontaneous guy. See a beautiful

3   girl ... she likes me ... I like her ... I'm going to kiss her.

4 ALEXIS: Really? I like that.

5 BOBBY: But to set it up in the choir room at twelve

6   hundred hours ... I don't know. Not my style.

7 JAKE: Can you two just stay out of this?

8 BOBBY: Just offering my thoughts.

9 ALEXIS: So, Bobby ... have you had much experience in the

10   kissing field?

11 BOBBY: Truthfully ... no.

12 ALEXIS: Me neither.

13 BOBBY: You've never been kissed?

14 ALEXIS: I'm afraid not.

15 BOBBY: Then that makes three of us.

16 REAGAN: Three of us?

17 BOBBY: Me, you, and Jake.

18 JAKE: Bobby!

19 BOBBY: Well, you told me you'd never kissed a girl. Except

20   for on her cheek or hand playing spin the bottle on a

21   choir trip.

22 JAKE: Thanks, Bobby.

23 ALEXIS: Then it makes four of us. Reagan hasn't kissed a

24   boy either.

25 JAKE: Really?

26 REAGAN: Really.

27 ALEXIS: Well, look at us!

28 JAKE: Reagan, if you don't want to ...

29 REAGAN: I do!

30 ALEXIS: Lunchtime in the choir room!

31 BOBBY: *(To ALEXIS)* Maybe we should go too.

32 JAKE: For what?

33 REAGAN: To watch?

34 ALEXIS: *(To BOBBY)* I'll go if you go.

35 BOBBY: There are several practice rooms in there.

1   ALEXIS: You mean ... ?

2   BOBBY: If you want.

3   ALEXIS: *(Smiling at him)* Yes. Maybe I would. We could all

4   experience our first kiss.

5   BOBBY: Great! Because I've been practicing.

6   JAKE: You have?

7   REAGAN: How?

8   BOBBY: My hand.

9   ALEXIS: So have I! *(Stops herself.)* I mean once. Just

10   wondering. You know, what it would be like.

11 BOBBY: It would be like this. *(Closes eyes and kisses hand*

12   *wildly.)*

13 ALEXIS: Wow.

14 REAGAN: It would be like that?

15 JAKE: Not like that, Bobby.

16 ALEXIS: You know, I don't think I'm ready for that first

17   kiss after all.

18 BOBBY: Not ready for a kiss like this? *(Kisses his hand*

19   *wildly again.)*

20 ALEXIS: No. I don't think so. I mean, I know so. No way am

21   I doing that.

22 REAGAN: *(To JAKE)* Is that the way you kiss, too?

23 JAKE: No. I mean, I don't think so. I mean, I've never ... you

24   know ... kissed before. Except a hand.

25 REAGAN: Me neither. But if it's like that .... *(Shakes head.)*

26 JAKE: Thanks, Bobby. Thanks a lot.

27 BOBBY: What? I thought girls wanted to be kissed like

28   that? Like in the movies.

29 ALEXIS: Not like that. That is too ... too everything.

30   Reagan, I have to go. See ya later. *(She exits.)*

31 REAGAN: But ...

32 BOBBY: *(To REAGAN)* Don't be nervous, Reagan. I've given

33   Jake lots of advice. Close your eyes ... tilt your head ...

34   then *powie!* Throw that kiss on her. Moving your

35   head all around like this ... *(Demonstrates.)* Getting all

1   slobbery ... maybe slipping in a little tongue action ...

2   REAGAN: *(Steps back.)* Oh, no! I'm not doing that.

3   JAKE: Bobby, you're such an idiot. No one kisses like that.

4   BOBBY: They do in the movies.

5   JAKE: We're not in the movies, Bobby.

6   BOBBY: But girls like romance. Isn't that romantic?

7   REAGAN: No! No it's not. Sorry, Jake. I promised to grab

8   lunch with Alexis at the snack bar. So I can't ... well ...

9   you know ... meet you in the choir room. Sorry. I've

10   got to go. *(Runs off.)*

11   JAKE: Way to go, Bobby. You just scared off both of the

12   girls.

13   BOBBY: What did I do?

14   JAKE: Your imitation of a first kiss was enough to make

15   me run, too. Now I don't even want to experience it.

16   Thanks, Bobby. Thanks a lot. *(Exits.)*

17   BOBBY: I don't get it. Hmmmm ... *(Thinking)* On second

18   thought, maybe the girls like it more soft and tender.

19   Yes, that's it. Soft and tender. Like this. *(Gives his*

20   *hand a quick kiss.)* Like that. Yes, that's it. That's what

21   the girls will like. Now I just have to practice. *(He exits,*

22   *kissing his hand.)*

About the Author

Laurie Allen was drawn to the theatre while performing plays under the legendary drama instructor, Jerry P. Worsham, at Snyder High School. In this small West Texas town, advancing to and winning the State UIL One-Act Competition in Austin was a goal often achieved. The drama department was hugely supported by the community and earned a reputation of respect and awe as they brought home many awards and first place trophies.

Following this experience, Laurie decided to try her hand at writing plays. Her first play, "Gutter Girl," won the Indian River Players Festival of One-Act Plays Competition. With that, she was hooked, knowing she had found her place in the theatre. Now, more than twenty-five of her plays have been published by various publishing companies. Her plays have been performed at many theatres including The Gettysburg College, The Globe of the Great Southwest, The American Theatre of Actors and the Paw Paw Village Players. Her plays for teens have enjoyed wide success with many going all the way to national speech and forensics competitions.

Laurie Allen may be contacted at txplaywright@aol.com.

Order Form

Meriwether Publishing Ltd.
PO Box 7710
Colorado Springs, CO 80933-7710
Phone: 800-937-5297 Fax: 719-594-9916
Website: www.meriwether.com

Please send me the following books:

_____	**33 Short Comedy Plays for Teens** **#BK-B325** by Laurie Allen *Plays for small casts*	**$17.95**
_____	**Comedy Plays and Scenes** **for Student Actors #BK-B320** by Laurie Allen *Short sketches for young performers*	**$17.95**
_____	**Comedy Scenes for Student Actors** **#BK-B308** by Laurie Allen *Short sketches for young performers*	**$17.95**
_____	**Sixty Comedy Duet Scenes for Teens** **#BK-B302** by Laurie Allen *Real-life situations for laughter*	**$17.95**
_____	**Thirty Short Comedy Plays for Teens** **#BK-B292** by Laurie Allen *Plays for a variety of cast sizes*	**$16.95**
_____	**Improv Ideas #BK-B283** by Justine Jones and Mary Ann Kelley *A book of games and lists*	**$23.95**
_____	**Acting Duets for Young Women** **#BK-B317** by Laurie Allen *8- to 10-minute duo scenes for practice and competition*	**$17.95**

These and other fine Meriwether Publishing books are available at your local bookstore or direct from the publisher. Prices subject to change without notice. Check our website or call for current prices.

Name: _____ email:_____

Organization name: _____

Address: _____

City: _____ State: _____

Zip: _____ Phone: _____

❑ **Check enclosed**

❑ **Visa / MasterCard / Discover / Am. Express #** _____

Signature: _____ *Expiration*
date: _____ / _____
(required for credit card orders)

Colorado residents: Please add 3% sales tax.
Shipping: Include $3.95 for the first book and 75¢ for each additional book ordered.

❑ *Please send me a copy of your complete catalog of books and plays.*